D0254519

Perfect Phrases *for* the TOEFL Speaking and Writing Sections

Perfect Phrases *for* the TOEFL Speaking and Writing Sections

Hundreds of Ready-to-Use Phrases to Improve Your Conversational Ability, Develop Your Writing Skills, and Build Exam Confidence

Roberta G. Steinberg

New York Chicago San Francisco Lisbon London
Madrid Mexico City Milan New Delhi San Juan
Seoul Singapore Sydney Toronto

1 2 3 4 5 6 7 8 9 0   DOC/DOC   0 9 8

ISBN: 978-0-07-159246-8
MHID: 0-07-159246-6

This book is printed on acid-free paper.

Contents

Contents

Contents

Perfect Phrases *for* the TOEFL Speaking and Writing Sections

Part I

Introduction: How to Use the Book

The TOEFL iBT (Internet-based Test) is different from previous TOEFL exams in that it includes a speaking section and an integrated writing section. Students who have taken the test have found these additional sections to be particularly difficult. Using this book will help you prepare for these two sections. You will become familiar with the types of tasks or prompts for each section. Each prompt in this book is followed by a response, which highlights the vocabulary and phrases you can use when you take the test. By studying the phrases and vocabulary organized by skill and purpose, you will gain confidence in your speaking and writing ability.

The book is divided into three sections: the speaking section, the writing section, and suggestions for vocabulary development. In the speaking and writing sections, you will learn what is tested on the IBT exam. The speaking section tests six different types of tasks. The writing section tests two different types of tasks. For each task, you will find:

- A description of the particular task you must perform.
- Two sample questions/lectures/conversations.

- Sample responses with note-taking suggestions and preparation tips.
- Phrases and vocabulary with reference to each type of task, organized by skill and purpose.

At the end of the listening section you will find a list of helpful Websites. As you prepare for the test by listening to native English speakers as well as by reading and writing every day, you will recognize the need to improve your vocabulary. The suggestions for vocabulary development section includes several time-tested strategies as well as the Academic Word List, a 300-word list of the most frequently used words in university lectures as compiled by Averil Coxhead.

At the end of the book are two appendixes, one a grammar section with rules and exercises and the other a punctuation section with rules. Several of the exercises include actual student errors. Each appendix has a pretest and posttest with answer keys that direct you to the particular rule being tested. These sections will help you prepare for the TOEFL writing and speaking sections. They will be of particular help with your writing.

Good luck on the exam and feel free to e-mail me with any questions or comments at *rgsteinberg@mountida.edu.*

Part II

The Speaking Section

Chapter 1 Description of Tasks

I n the speaking section you will answer six questions while you are speaking into a microphone. The first two tasks are the easiest. They are about topics that are familiar to you. These topics are called *independent tasks*. One will be a personal preference, and one will be a paired choice, a question that asks you to make and defend a choice between two different behaviors. The third and fourth tasks, *integrated tasks*, involve listening, reading, and speaking. One of these tasks is about a campus-based situation, and the other involves an academic topic. The fifth and sixth *integrated tasks* integrate listening and speaking skills. Again, one is campus-based, while the other is academic.

You will take notes to help you prepare for your responses. You will be given a short amount of time, between 15 and 30 seconds, to prepare your responses. You will speak for either 45 or 60 seconds. A clock on the computer shows the time.

A. Independent Task: Speaking, Personal Preference

You will hear a single question that asks you to express and defend a choice from a given category, for example, people, places, events, or activities. Your answer will express your opinion, and you will be expected to provide the reasons that support your opinion.

1. Sample Prompt with Response

■ *Here is the kind of question you will be asked:*

If you could visit any foreign country in the world for two weeks, all expenses paid, which country would it be and why?

---

15 seconds preparation time; 45 seconds to speak

■ *In the 15 seconds of preparation time, you could write down the bulleted items shown below to help you get ready to respond.*

Preparation Notes

Although a country may not come to mind right away, just pick one. Don't waste valuable time trying to find a "best" choice. Any country will work as long as you have specific reasons for wanting

Description of Tasks

to go there. Once you choose, start listing in bullet form the particulars. The more specific and detailed your answer is, the better it will be.

- *Where? India*
- *Why?*
- *Differences: smells, food, appearance, customs, religion, way of life*
- *How it might change my life*

This speaking task is the easiest one. Watch the clock to make sure you don't go over the time limit.

- **Here is a sample response. <u>Underlined</u> words and phrases are categorized in Chapter 2, Phrases and Vocabulary for the Speaking Section with Reference to Skill and Purpose.**

<u>Let's see</u> **(S1)**. <u>That's an interesting question</u> **(S1)**. <u>If I could</u> **(S3)** travel to one country for free, <u>I believe</u> **(S2)** I'd go to India. <u>I'd like to explain why</u> **(S2)**. <u>First of all</u> **(S4)**, India is very different from where I have always lived. <u>Personally</u> **(S2)**, <u>I'd enjoy</u> **(S2)** visiting a country with such exotic customs, appearances, smells, and food. <u>In addition</u> **(S4)**, I'd have the chance to observe people whose religion, beliefs

---

and practices are ones I know very little about. <u>Even if</u> **(S3)** the visit were a short one, I'm sure it would be eye-opening. <u>To summarize</u> **(S5)**, <u>if I could</u> **(S3)** go to India, <u>I'd be able to</u> **(S6)** experience a nation that is unlike any I've ever known. <u>Above all</u> **(S11)**, I'm sure that <u>as a result</u> **(S7)** <u>I'd be capable of</u> **(S6)** thinking about things differently.

2. Sample Prompt with Response

◾ *Here is the kind of question you will be asked:*

If you could have any job, what would it be and why?

15 seconds preparation time; 45 seconds to speak

◾ *In the 15 seconds of preparation time, you could write down the bulleted items shown below to help you get ready to respond.*

Preparation Notes

You may not have any idea of what you might consider an ideal job, but just quickly pick a job. Any job, as long as you have specific reasons for why you would like it, will work. Once you choose, start listing in bullet form the particulars. The more specific and detailed your answer is, the better it will be.

Description of Tasks

- *The job. A doctor*
- *Why?*
- *Help people*
- *Respected profession*
- *Make a good living*
- *Never routine*

Watch the clock to make sure you don't go over the time limit.

- ***Here is a sample response. <u>Underlined</u> words and phrases are categorized in Chapter 2, Phrases and Vocabulary for the Speaking Section with Reference to Skill and Purpose.***

<u>Let me think</u> (**S1**). <u>That's a good question</u> (**S1**). <u>If I could</u> (**S3**) have any job, <u>I think</u> (**S2**) <u>I'd enjoy</u> (**S2**) being a doctor. <u>As far as I'm concerned</u> (**S2**), a doctor <u>certainly</u> (**S11**) is   <u>not only</u> (**S13**) respected <u>but also</u> (**S13**) <u>able</u> (**S6**) to positively affect the lives of many people. <u>Every day</u> (**S8**) a doctor sees different patients and must make life-altering decisions. <u>On the whole</u> (**S6**), the job is <u>never</u> (**S8**) routine or boring, <u>for</u> (**S17**) no two patients are alike. <u>Furthermore</u> (**S4**), a doctor must keep learning new things. <u>In spite of</u> (**S10**) the demands, a doctor remains challenged <u>as well as</u> (**S16**) motivated. <u>What's more</u> (**S4**), a physician makes a lot of money, <u>compensation for</u> (**S17**) the many years of study and grueling hours. <u>Unquestionably</u> (**S10**), <u>I'd be</u> (**S2**) a doctor <u>if I could</u> (**S3**) choose any job.

B.   Independent Task: Paired Choice Task

You will hear a single question that asks you to make and defend a choice between two different behaviors. Your answer will express your opinion, and you will be expected to provide the reasons behind your opinions. The question is personal in nature.

1. Sample Prompt with Response

■ *Here is the kind of question you will be asked:*

Some high schools require all students to wear a uniform to school. Other schools allow students to wear whatever they want. Which policy do you think is better and why?

---

15 seconds preparation time; 45 seconds to speak

■ *In the 15 seconds of preparation time, you could write down the bulleted items shown below to help you get ready to respond.*

Preparation Notes

Although you may not have an opinion about which policy is better, you'll need to quickly make up your mind. Brainstorm your ideas in two columns, and again list bulleted specifics.

Description of Tasks

With Uniforms
- _Cheaper, don't need many outfits_
- _Promotes equality_
- _Promotes school identification/ belonging_

Without Uniforms
- _Fosters individuality_
- _Fosters originality_

Maybe you don't have an opinion. Since you have more reasons for wearing a uniform, choose that side. What's important is to act quickly. Just as in an essay, you'll have an introduction, supporting evidence, and a conclusion. Watch the clock; 45 seconds goes by quickly.

- **_Here is a sample response. <u>Underlined</u> words and phrases are categorized in Chapter 2, Phrases and Vocabulary for the Speaking Section with Reference to Skill and Purpose._**

<u>Whether to</u> **(S3)** allow high school students to choose what they wear to school <u>is an interesting question</u> **(S1)** <u>because</u> **(S7)** everyone has been to high school and has thought about this issue. <u>There are three reasons</u> **(S4)** <u>why I believe</u> **(S2)** students should wear uniforms. <u>First</u> **(S4)**, you don't have to worry about what to wear each day. <u>Second</u> **(S4)**, when everyone is wearing the same thing, no one appears richer or poorer than anyone else based on clothing. <u>Finally</u> **(S5)**, and <u>most importantly</u> **(S5)**, wearing a uniform promotes camaraderie and identification with a school. <u>In conclusion</u> **(S5)**, <u>although</u> **(S10)** <u>some may argue that</u> **(S10)** not wearing a uniform promotes freedom of expression and individuality, <u>overall</u> **(S9)**, the ease and sense of belonging by wearing a uniform <u>makes it a better policy</u> **(S15)**.

2. Sample Prompt with Response

■ *Here is the kind of question you will be asked:*

Some students prefer to take online courses. Others prefer to study in a classroom with a live teacher. Which do you think is better and why?

---

15 seconds preparation time; 45 seconds to speak

■ **In the 15 seconds of preparation time, you could write down the bulleted points shown below to help you get ready to respond.**

Preparation Notes

Although you may not have an opinion about which option is better, you'll need to quickly make up your mind. Brainstorm your ideas in two columns, and again list bulleted specifics.

Online	In a Classroom
■ Can do the course in pajamas whenever	■ Can ask the teacher ques.
■ Can go at my speed/ repeat lectures	■ Can learn from other students/can meet with them after class
■ Don't spend time commuting	

Description of Tasks

Maybe you don't have a strong opinion, but since you have more reasons for taking online courses, choose that side. What's important is to act quickly. Just as in an essay, you'll have an introduction, supporting evidence, and a conclusion. Watch the clock; 45 seconds goes by quickly.

■ *Here is a sample response. <u>Underlined</u> words and phrases are categorized in Chapter 2, Phrases and Vocabulary for the Speaking Section with Reference to Skill and Purpose.*

There are two ways to take college courses. <u>One option is</u> **(S20)** to take the course online. <u>The other option is</u> **(S1)** to take the course in a traditional college classroom. <u>Although</u> **(S10)** <u>there are benefits</u> **(S13)** to both, <u>it seems to me</u> **(S2)** that taking a course online <u>might be the better option</u> **(S15)**. <u>First</u> **(S4)**, I can decide <u>when</u> **(S8)** to go online, which may be <u>while</u> **(S8)** I'm lying in bed or even in my pajamas. <u>Second</u> **(S4)**, <u>if</u> **(S3)** I need to replay the lecture, <u>I'm able to</u> **(S6)** <u>as many times as</u> **(S16)** needed. <u>Finally</u> **(S5)**, I don't have to get dressed and commute to a classroom, which might take a very long time. <u>Even though</u> **(S10)** <u>others may argue</u> **(S14)** that taking a course in a classroom <u>enables</u> **(S6)** interaction with teachers and students, <u>on the whole</u> **(S5)** for me, taking a class online <u>is the better option</u> **(S15)**.

C. Integrated Task: Reading/Listening/ Speaking (*Campus-based*)

You will read a passage of between 75 and 100 words regarding a campus issue. You will then hear a conversation of approximately 150–180 words discussing the passage. The question asks you to summarize what you read and then discuss one of the speaker's opinions. You will need to integrate the written and spoken information.

1. Sample Prompt with Response

▪ *Here is the kind of passage you will read followed immediately by a related conversation you will hear. Take notes on what you read and what you hear.*

Narrator: You will read a message from a college president about a change in when tuition bills must be paid. You have 45 seconds to read the message. Begin now.

MESSAGE FROM THE PRESIDENT

Beginning with the fall semester, tuition bills must be paid in full before classes begin. Returning students will not be able to attend classes for which they preregistered last spring if there is an outstanding balance due on the account. Although in previous semesters students were allowed to attend classes if 50 percent of the bill was paid, the new policy, with no exceptions, will go into effect immediately. The bursar's office is open Monday to Friday from nine to six to assist you with financial aid, loans, and scholarship applications. Please check your account balance online.

> ■ *In the 45 seconds you have to read the passage, you could write down the following (notice that the notes are in abbreviated form to save time; 45 seconds to read and take notes is a very short time):*
> ■ *New policy: 100% paid bef. attending class.*
> ■ *Old policy: only 50% nded be pd.*

Narrator: Now listen to two students discuss the message.

Woman: Did you get the e-mail about the new tuition policy?

Man: Yeah. I'm pretty upset about it. In the past I had worked out a payment plan and paid what I owed monthly.

Woman: I don't know what I'm going to do.

Man: I wish they had given us more notice. I may have to take out another loan or even drop out of school. I should have taken a second job over the summer instead of doing that unpaid internship.

Woman: Don't be sorry about that. You know that the internship is really going to pay off in your future job search.

Man: Yeah, if I can afford to graduate. I can understand why they want the money up front, but I wonder how many students are going to have to leave the college altogether.

Woman: Maybe we should organize a petition drive.

Man: Let's do something on a smaller scale. Come with me to the bursar's office. We're already seniors, and this new policy wasn't in effect when we started. Let's see if seniors can be exempt.

■ *While listening, you could write down:*

Man objects: was on payment plan, now a senior, wants exemption, wasn't paid last summer, would have taken a job

---

Narrator: What is the new college policy? Why does the man object to the policy? Explain why he thinks his suggestion should be considered.

---

30 seconds preparation time; 60 seconds to speak

■ *In the 30 seconds of preparation time, you could write down the points shown below—using your reading and listening notes—to help you get ready to respond.*

Preparation Notes

Looking at notes from reading and listening, you can brainstorm the following points.

Description of Tasks

New Policy	_Man's Objections_	_His Suggestion_
▪ 100% due before classes	▪ senior, too late to get money, no notice, wouldn't have done unpaid internship	▪ exempt seniors, policy hadn't been in place

Watch the clock. 60 seconds is longer than the time you had for the previous tasks. Make sure you answer all three parts of the question: the policy, the man's objections, and why he thinks his suggestion should be considered.

▪ **Here is a sample response. <u>Underlined</u> words and phrases will be categorized in Chapter 2, Phrases and Vocabulary for the Speaking Section with Reference to Skill and Purpose.**

The new college <u>policy is that</u> **(S12)** all students must pay their tuition bills in full <u>before</u> **(S8)** classes begin <u>even though</u> **(S10)** in the past students could attend <u>if</u> **(S3)** half of the bill had been paid by the beginning of the school year. The man <u>objects</u> **(S14)** <u>because</u> **(S7)** until this year he had paid the remainder of his tuition monthly <u>after</u> **(S8)** classes began. He <u>contends</u> **(S13)** that he didn't have enough notice to get a paying job over the summer and <u>instead</u> **(S10)** did

---

17

an unpaid internship. His suggestion **(S13)** is to exempt seniors, like him, from the new policy since **(S7)** the policy was not in place when he began as a student. Because **(S7)** he wasn't given any notice, he feels **(S2)** that his suggestion is valid **(S13)** and will go to speak to someone in the bursar's office to plead **(S13)** his case immediately **(S8)**.

2. Sample Prompt with Response

■ *Here is the kind of passage you will read followed immediately by a related conversation you will hear. Take notes on what you read and what you hear.*

Narrator: **You will read a message from the Office of Student Affairs about applying to live in a new residence hall. You have 45 seconds to read the message. Begin now.**

E-MAIL FROM THE OFFICE OF STUDENT AFFAIRS

We are pleased to announce that our new residence hall, Shaw Hall, will be ready for occupancy this fall. This state-of-the-art facility includes a kitchen for every four rooms, a dance studio, music practice rooms, a theater in the round, and numerous study areas. Other amenities include a fitness center, air-conditioning, and several elevators. Because of popular demand, only seniors may apply. Since we anticipate that demand will be greater than the space available, interested students must submit an application including a transcript, honors and awards, participation in extracurricular activities, and a teacher recommendation.

- *In the 45 seconds you have to read the passage, you could write down the following (notice the notes are in abbreviated form to save time; 45 seconds to read and take notes is a very short time):*
- *New dorm: seniors only, kitch, thr., elev. AC*
- *App: GPA, ldshp, extra curr.*

Narrator: Now listen to two students discuss the message.

Woman: Did you get the e-mail about the new dorm?

Man: Yeah. I didn't believe it would be ready for this fall.

Woman: So, you're going to submit an application, aren't you?

Man: Of course, but I'm a little worried. My GPA is okay, but I don't have any awards or honors to list.

Woman: What about extracurricular?

Man: Well, I'm on the lacrosse team. All those hours of practice and games should count for something.

Woman: Sure. However, I assume what they're really looking for are the class president, you know, student government positions. Maybe I'm wrong.

Man: Oh well. I do play the clarinet. I can put down that I need a practice room.

Woman: Good luck. I hope we're dormmates.

■ *While listening, you could write down:*

Man: OK GPA but no awd/hon. Plays lacrosse/clarinet, no stud.govt. pos.

Narrator: What is included in the new dorm application? Why is the man nervous about his chances? Explain why he thinks he may qualify.

---

30 seconds preparation time; 60 seconds to speak

■ *In the 30 seconds of preparation time, you could write down the points shown below—using your reading and listening notes—to help you get ready to respond.*

Preparation Notes

Looking at notes from reading and listening, you can brainstorm the following points.

Application	Why Nervous	May Qualify
■ GPA	■ No Awd/Hon	■ Lacrosse
■ Extracurr.		■ Clarinet
■ Hon/Awds		

Description of Tasks

Watch the clock. 60 seconds is longer than the time you had for the previous tasks. Make sure you answer all three parts of the question: the application, why the man is nervous, why he thinks he may qualify.

■ **Here is a sample response. _Underlined_ words and phrases are categorized in Chapter 2, Phrases and Vocabulary for the Speaking Section with Reference to Skill and Purpose.**

In order to **(S17)** apply for a space in the new dormitory, rising seniors must <u>both</u> **(S13)** fill out an application, including their GPA, list honors and awards, extracurricular activities, <u>and</u> **(S13)** submit a teacher recommendation. The man is nervous <u>because</u> **(S7)** he has <u>neither</u> **(S10)** honors <u>nor</u> **(S10)** awards to list. Furthermore **(S4)**, his GPA is okay, but it doesn't sound <u>as though</u> **(S3)** it's outstanding. <u>However</u> **(S10)**, he hopes that his being a member of the lacrosse team, having spent many hours practicing <u>as well as</u> **(S16)** playing games, <u>in addition to</u> **(S18)** playing the clarinet, will <u>then</u> **(S5)** offset the lack of honors and awards. To <u>summarize</u> **(S5)**, he hopes his endeavors <u>enable</u> **(S6)** him to live in the new dorm.

D. Integrated Task: Listening/Reading/ Speaking (*Academic Topic*)

You will read a passage of approximately 75–100 words that gives background information about an academic subject. You will then hear part of a 150–220 word lecture that deals with the subject. You will then analyze how what you heard is related to what you read.

1. Sample Prompt with Response

■ *Here is the kind of passage you will read followed immediately by a related lecture you will hear. Take notes on what you read and what you hear.*

Narrator: Read the passage about personal space. You have 45 seconds to read the passage.

One way that people can communicate is by manipulating space. People have a very strong sense of personal space that surrounds them. Edward T. Hall studied attitudes toward physical proximity in several cultures. He found that different peoples vary in the degree of closeness they accept from strangers or acquaintances, with Americans requiring more personal space than any other group—at least 30 to 36 inches. Americans traveling to other countries find that the inhabitants stand almost offensively close. People in these cultures often consider Americans—who are always retreating when they try to talk to them—rude.

> ■ ***In the 45 seconds you have to read the passage, you could write down:***
>
> ■ *Peo: strg. sense of space around*
> ■ *Hall stud. spc.*
> ■ *Amers. need most: 30–36", noticeable when trav.*

Narrator: Now listen to part of a lecture on the same topic in a sociology class.

Professor: You've all read Chapter 10 which describes Edward Hall's work on personal space, the distance one keeps from another person in public. I'm sure you found what he had to say about Americans interesting and important. A friend of mine recently traveled to another continent for the first time. I'm not going to tell you which one, but I'm sure you can guess.

From the minute she got off the plane, she couldn't believe how everyone seemed to be talking in her face. She felt extremely uncomfortable and found herself backing away whenever anyone started talking to her. She hadn't been prepared for total strangers putting their arms on her shoulders or giving her hugs and kisses. Once someone explained to her that what is normal in the United States—a personal space of 30 to 36 inches—is actually *half* the distance where she was visiting, she was able to make some accommodations in her own behavior and be less critical.

Although this example is a social one, we'll be discussing the implications of Hall's work in world trade and diplomacy.

▨ ***While listening you could write down:***

▨ *Prof's friend travl.*

▨ *Felt uncomf: people too close, hugs, kisses*

▨ *Learned about sense of sp.*

▨ *Implications*

Narrator: **The professor describes a woman's travels. How does what you read support what you heard?**

---

30 seconds preparation time; 60 seconds to speak

▨ ***In the 30 seconds of preparation time, you could write down the items shown below—using your reading and listening notes—to help you get ready to respond.***

Preparation Notes

Looking at notes from reading and listening, you can brainstorm the following points.

<u>Reading</u>   <u>Lecture</u>

▨ *Hall studied sp. Amers.*   ▨ *Woman, Am, traveled abr. nded sp.*
need most 30–36"   ▨ *Objected to dist. and beh.*
                                   ▨ *Once she understd. More accepting*

Watch the clock. 60 seconds of speaking time is longer than the time you had for some of the earlier tasks. Make sure you explain the connection between what you read and what you heard.

Description of Tasks

■ *Here is a sample response. <u>Underlined</u> words and phrases are categorized in Chapter 2, Phrases and Vocabulary for the Speaking Section with Reference to Skill and Purpose.*

Edward T. Hall studied the behavior of different cultures regarding personal space, finding that Americans require the greatest distance—30 to 36 inches. <u>This observation is supported by</u> **(S13)** the professor's American friend <u>when</u> **(S8)** she traveled abroad. <u>Just as</u> **(S16)** Hall observed, this woman felt very uncomfortable <u>as</u> **(S8)** she traveled to an area of the world whose inhabitants stand much closer than Americans do and who are more affectionate with strangers than Americans are. <u>As soon as</u> **(S8)** she understood what was considered to be normal behavior in the area, she modified her behavior and criticisms. The lecturer used his friend's trip <u>as evidence of</u> **(S18)** <u>the legitimacy of</u> **(S18)** Hall's work.

---

2. Sample Prompt with Response

■ *Here is the kind of passage you will read followed immediately by a related lecture you will hear. Take notes on what you read and what you hear.*

Narrator: Read the passage about camouflage. You have 45 seconds to read the passage.

The word camouflage, comes from the French, *camoufler*, meaning to disguise. In nature, animals blend into their environment, concealing their presence to avoid predators. One method is to attach to natural materials for concealment. Some herd animals, such as zebras, have patterns which make distinguishing a single animal difficult. The most common form of camouflage is to be of a color similar to the surroundings, such as earth tones of deer and squirrels. Some animals change colors in different seasons, such as the Artic fox whose white coat in winter changes to brown in the summer.

- *In the 45 seconds you have to read the passage, you could write down:*
- *Camou. to disguise*
- *Used by animals*
- *Blending, changing colors*

Narrator: **Now listen to part of a lecture on the same topic in a history class.**

Professor: As we've discussed, camouflage has long been a fascinating occurrence in nature. For millions of years of natural selection, those species able to avoid their predators, with the help of camouflage, have survived.

Today we're going to discuss the use of camouflage in the military. Surprisingly, even in the 1800s, armies tended to wear bright colors with bold impressive designs, to irritate the enemy, attract recruits, foster solidarity, and allow for easy identification.

Description of Tasks

Only in 1857 because of high casualties did the British, fighting in India, dye their tunics neutral tones, initially a muddy tan called *khaki* from the Urdu word for dusty. Other armies followed suit, either with khaki or with other colors suitable for their environments.

Today's camouflage is not only customized for terrain, weather, and light conditions but also symbolizes the national identity for the military. Newly independent nations immediately put their own design on camouflage patterns. As technology advances, modern camouflage must take into account infrared and thermal vision. What has been noticeable for several decades is the popularity of camouflage-influenced articles of clothing among the general population.

■ *While listening you could write down:*

■ *Cam. in the military*

■ *Bold colors until mid–1800s*

■ *Brit. deaths forced change to khaki*

■ *Changing tod. to reflect tech.*

■ *Pop. as clothing items*

> **Narrator: The professor describes camouflage in the military. How does what you read support what you heard?**

30 seconds preparation time; 60 seconds to speak

- **In the 30 seconds of preparation time, you could write down the information shown below—using your reading and listening notes—to help you get ready to respond.**

Preparation Notes

While looking at your notes from reading and listening, you can brainstorm the following points.

<u>Reading</u>	<u>Lecture</u>
■ Animals-camouflage to survive	■ *Not until mid 1800s*
	■ *British finally adopted cam. unif.*
■ *Millions of years*	■ *Evolving even today*

Watch the clock. 60 seconds of speaking time is longer than the time you had for some of the earlier tasks Make sure you explain the connection between what you read and what you heard.

- **Here is a sample response. <u>Underlined</u> words and phrases are categorized in Chapter 2, Phrases and Vocabulary for the Speaking Section with Reference to Skill and Purpose.**

The reading passage describes the evolutionary development of camouflage as used by animals. <u>In order to</u> **(S17)** avoid capture, animals either blend in with their environment or change color. The lecturer <u>then</u> **(S8)** chronicles the relatively recent use of camouflage by the military. Curiously (S10), in the case of (S18) armies, humans have been much slower to use camouflage. Not until (S10) the mid 1800s, due to (S7) high casualties, did the British finally (S5) abandon their brightly colored uniforms in favor of (S4) khaki ones which blended in with the environment. Just as (S16) animals continue to adapt in their use of camouflage, in the same way (S16) military uniforms must change as (S8) technology evolves.

E. Integrated Task: Listening/Speaking (*Campus-based*)

You will hear a passage of approximately 180–220 words. It will be a conversation about a student-related problem and two possible solutions. You will need to understand the problem and give your opinion as to the better solution.

■ *Here is the kind of conversation you will hear, followed immediately by a question. Take notes as you listen.*

1. Sample Prompt with Response

Narrator: **Listen to a conversation between a student and her advisor.**

(**KNOCK KNOCK**)

Woman: Professor Martin? It's Stephanie Martinez, your advisee.

Man: Oh, come in, Stephanie. What can I do for you?

Woman: You know I'm a junior econ. major. I've been doing some investigating, and I've found that many investment firms, ones I hope to work for, prefer students with excellent writing skills. If I could get a dual degree with English, I'd be more employable.

Man: That's certainly commendable, but isn't it a little late?

Woman: Actually, I've always enjoyed English classes, and I have already taken several as open electives.

Man: Well, there are two issues you need to think about. One is whether you have enough open electives to fulfill all the English requirements, and two is whether all the remaining courses you need for both majors will be offered in the next year and a half and at the times you'll be able to take them.

Woman: I've done my homework. I'm actually not too far behind. I'll need only two additional courses. I have two options. I can take six courses instead of five both semesters senior year or two courses in summer school this summer.

Man: But you'd have to pay for summer school.

Woman: I know, but it's deciding what's worse, 12 courses senior year instead of 10 or the added expense of summer school.

- *While listening, you could write down:*
- *Problem: Adding English major*
- *Go to summer school*
- *Take 6 courses not 5 each sem. Sen. Yr.*

Description of Tasks

> **Narrator:** The student describes two solutions to her problem. Describe the problem and then tell which of the two solutions you would prefer and why.

20 seconds preparation time; 60 seconds to speak

- **In the 20 seconds of preparation time, you could write down the information shown below—using your listening notes—to help you get ready to respond.**

Preparation Notes

<u>Solution 1</u>	<u>Solution 2</u>	<u>My Choice</u>
Pay for summer school	Take 6 courses, not 5 each semester senior Yr.	Additional courses sen.yr. b/c of money, if money no prob.SS

Watch the clock. 20 seconds of preparation is less time than you had for the tasks that include listening and reading. 60 seconds of speaking time is longer than the time you had for some of the earlier tasks but the same amount as the listening/reading task. Make sure you answer the two parts of the question: describe the problem and which solution you prefer.

- **Here is a sample response. <u>Underlined</u> words and phrases are categorized in Chapter 2, Phrases and Vocabulary for the Speaking Section with Reference to Skill and Purpose.**

Stephanie, a junior econ. major would now like to obtain an English degree as well. <u>The problem is how</u> **(S19)** she'll be able to fit in the required courses in the year and a half she has left before she graduates. <u>She is considering two options</u> **(S20)**. <u>One option is</u> **(S20)** to take six courses instead of five both semesters her senior year. <u>The other option is</u> **(S20)** to take the two needed courses in summer school. <u>Because</u> **(S7)** she would have to pay to go to summer school, <u>I would prefer</u> **(S2)** her taking the 12 courses her senior year. <u>Although</u> **(S10)** summer school <u>might be an easier option</u> **(S20)**, the additional expense <u>seems to warrant</u> **(S13)** the senior year overload. <u>On the other hand</u> **(S10)**, if money is not a concern, <u>then</u> **(S5)** going to summer school <u>may be the better option</u> **(S15)**.

2. Sample Prompt with Response

Narrator: Listen to a conversation from advisor to advisor.

(KNOCK KNOCK)

Man: Dean Curtis? It's Alex Manning. I have a two o'clock appointment.

Woman: You're a little early, but I'm free. Have you decided on your study-abroad destination yet?

Man: The last time we talked I told you that I couldn't decide between the semester at sea program or doing a semester in a university in Cairo.

Description of Tasks

Woman: Have you decided?

Man: The applications are due by the end of the month, and I'm still undecided.

Woman: Tell me what you like about each program.

Man: The semester at sea has several advantages. First, I love ships and sailing. I'd get to stop at 10 different ports and see many different countries. But, Cairo is also appealing. I'm an archaeology major, and I'd be able to spend quality time at the Pyramids. I've been studying Arabic, and I know that six months of living there would really improve my fluency.

Woman: And the negatives?

Man: Hmm... The only negative is that I can't do both!

- *While listening, you could write down:*
- *Problem: Deciding where to go abroad*
- *Sem. At sea/10 ports*
- *Sem. In Cairo: pyramids, Arabic*

Narrator: **The student describes two semester-abroad alternatives. Describe the two alternatives, and then tell which one you would prefer and why.**

---

20 seconds preparation time; 60 seconds to speak

- ***In the 20 seconds of preparation time, you could write down the information below—using your listening notes—to help you get ready to respond.***

Preparation Notes

Option 1	*Option 2*	*My Choice*
▪ *Semester at sea*	▪ *Cairo*	▪ *Cairo*
▪ *Different ports/loves ships*	▪ *Pyramids/Arabic*	▪ *Seasickness*

Watch the clock. 20 seconds of preparation is less time than you have for the tasks that include listening and reading. 60 seconds of speaking time is longer than the time you had for some of the earlier tasks but the same amount as the listening/reading task. Make sure that you answer the two parts of the question: describe the alternatives and which choice you prefer.

▪ ***Here is a sample response. <u>Underlined</u> words and phrases are categorized in Chapter 2, Phrases and Vocabulary for the Speaking Section with Reference to Skill and Purpose.***

The student <u>has two alternatives</u> **(S20)** for his semester abroad and is having trouble deciding which one <u>is the better alternative</u> **(S15)**. <u>On the one hand</u> **(S10)**, <u>he could</u> **(S6)** spend a semester at sea. He likes sailing; <u>furthermore</u> **(S4)**, <u>he'd be able</u> **(S6)** to visit many different countries. <u>On the other hand</u> **(S10)**, <u>he could</u> **(S6)** go to Cairo. <u>Not only</u> **(S13)** is he an archaeology major, <u>but</u> **(S13)** he's <u>also</u> **(S13)** been studying Arabic. His Arabic would <u>certainly</u> **(S11)** improve by living six months in Cairo. <u>In my opinion</u> **(S2)**,

➡

> I'd prefer (**S2**) to go to Cairo. There are three reasons (**S4**). First (**S4**), I get seasick. Second (**S4**), I'm also (**S13**) interested in archaeology. And third (**S4**), above all (**S11**) I'd prefer (**S2**) to get to know one country rather than (**S10**) making short stops at many destinations.

F. Integrated Task: Listening/Speaking (*Academic Topic*)

You will hear a passage from a lecture of approximately 230–280 words that explains a term or concept and gives one or two examples. You will summarize the lecture using examples that demonstrate an understanding of the topic.

- *Here is the kind of lecture you will hear, followed immediately by a question. While you're listening, take notes on what you hear.*

1. Sample Prompt with Response

Narrator: Now listen to part of a talk in a biology class.

Today's lecture concerns disorders and the sex chromosome. All humans have 23 pairs of chromosomes. A chromosome is the part of the cell that contains genetic information. The only difference between men and women is in one of those pairs, called the *sex chromosome*. For this 23rd chromosome pair, women have two X chromosomes, while men have one X and one Y.

Why do some disorders occur more often in men than in women? When a disorder is caused by a mutation or change on one of the 22 other chromosomes, the disorder will appear as often in men and women, ignoring other possible factors. But when a disorder occurs because of a mutation on the X chromosome, men are usually affected.

Why would a change in the X chromosome affect men more than woman if women have two Xs and men only one? Take colorblindness, which occurs when a cell is missing the gene needed to create a protein that differentiates colors. This gene regularly appears on the X chromosome. If a woman inherits two Xs, one without the gene and one with, she can still distinguish colors because she had one copy of the gene, which is enough. However, a man has only one X chromosome. If that one is missing the gene, he cannot differentiate certain colors.

Another example is hemophilia, a blood clotting disorder. It's caused by a defect in one of the genes located on the X chromosome. Because only the X chromosome carries the genes related to clotting factors, a man with the abnormal gene on his X chromosome will be affected. A female must have the gene on both of her X chromosomes, a very rare occurrence.

- *** While listening, you could write down***
- * *23rd pair: sex chromosome*
- * *Women 2X, men X+Y*
- * *When a male X is damaged/mutated-diseases occur.*

Narrator: Using points and examples from the talk, explain why colorblindness and hemophilia occur more often in men than in women.

Description of Tasks

20 seconds preparation time; 60 seconds to speak

- **In the 20 seconds of preparation time, you could write down the following—using your listening notes—to help you get ready to respond.**

Preparation Notes

- *CB + Hem. are sex-linked disorders*
- *Sex-linked based on the 23rd chromosome pr.*
- *Women 2X, Men X+Y, so if one of M's X is damaged, then certain disorders occur, whereas women have another X*

Watch the clock. 20 seconds of preparation is less time than you have for the tasks that include listening and reading. 60 seconds of speaking time is longer than the time you had for some of the earlier tasks but the same amount you had for the listening/reading task. Make sure you explain why colorblindness and hemophilia occur more often in men than in women.

- **Here is a sample response. <u>Underlined</u> words and phrases are categorized in Chapter 2, Phrases and Vocabulary for the Speaking Section with Reference to Skill and Purpose.**

Humans have 23 pairs of chromosomes—the cell parts that hold genetic information. There are some disorders, <u>such as</u> **(S18)** colorblindness and hemophilia, that occur <u>because of</u> **(S7)** a mutation in the X chromosome. <u>If</u> **(S3)** one of a woman's X chromosomes is damaged or missing, she has another X chromosome to compensate. <u>On the other hand</u> **(S10)**, if a man's X is damaged or missing, he will inherit the condition. <u>To sum up</u> **(S5)**, <u>because</u> **(S7)** women have two X chromosomes, they can compensate <u>if</u> **(S3)** one of them is missing or damaged, <u>whereas</u> **(S10)** men cannot. <u>As a result</u> **(S5)**, they are more likely to inherit sex-linked diseases <u>such as</u> **(S18)** hemophilia and colorblindness.

2. Sample Prompt with Response

Narrator: Now listen to part of a talk in an astronomy class.

The "dog days of summer" are periods of exceptionally hot and muggy weather that occur in July and August. The origin of the phrase describing these stifling, humid days is found in the stars.

Centuries ago, when artificial lights and pollution did not obscure the night sky, people in different areas around the world would look into the night sky and see a group of stars; then they would connect the dots. Over 2,000 years ago, Greek astronomers saw the same patterns in the northern sky as we see today. They named the star patterns, or *constellations*, after gods, mythological creatures, and animals familiar to them, such as the bears: Ursa Major and Ursa Minor. The dogs are called Canis Major and Canis Minor. The brightest of the stars in the big dog, Canis Major, is Sirius, which is the brightest star in the night sky.

Description of Tasks

During the summer, the dog star Sirius rises and sets with the sun. In late July, Sirius is aligned with the sun. The ancient Romans, Greeks, and Egyptians therefore mistakenly assumed that Sirius's heat intensified the heat of the sun, causing hotter days on Earth. They named this hot stretch—from 20 days before and after the alignment—"the dog days." Many people become sluggish at this time of year, and the ancients blamed Sirius for their discomfort.

It is easy to understand why the ancients felt that it was necessary to seek out a "scientific" explanation for extreme weather. We now know, however, that the heat during the warmest period of the summer is not caused by additional radiation from the dog star.

- *While listening, you could write down:*
- *Summer hot dog days/anci.Grks.*
- *Thought dog star made earth hotter*
- *Not true, of course*

Narrator: Using points and examples from the talk, explain why ancient Greeks coined the phrase "dog says of summer."

---

20 seconds preparation time; 60 seconds to speak

- *In the 20 seconds of preparation time, you could write down the information shown below—using your listening notes—to help you get ready to respond.*

Preparation Notes

- *Dog days: July/Aug.*
- *Greeks named stars after animals, brightest star: dog Sirius*
- *Thought Sirius caused sun to make Earth hotter, not true*

Watch the clock. 20 seconds of preparation is less time than you have for the tasks that include listening and reading. 60 seconds of speaking time is longer than the time you had for some of the earlier tasks but the same amount as for the listening/reading task. Make sure you answer why ancient Greeks coined the phrase "dog days of summer."

- **Here is a sample response. <u>Underlined</u> words and phrases are categorized in Preparation Notes.**

The ancient Greeks <u>mistakenly</u> **(S10)** believed that stars could effect the Sun. They named two constellations after dogs <u>because</u> **(S10)** the stars seemed to form the outlines of dogs. They believed that summer heat was <u>due to</u> **(S7)** the brightest star in these constellations, Sirius. <u>Because</u> **(S7)** Sirius was so bright, the Greeks <u>concluded</u> **(S5)** that it caused the Sun to be brighter. <u>As a result</u> **(S5)**, they named the hot July and August period dog days. <u>Obviously</u> **(S11)** today we know that the star Sirius does not cause any additional heat; <u>however</u> **(S10)**, we still use the term "dog days" to describe hot, lazy summer days.

Chapter 2 Phrases and Vocabulary for the Speaking Section with Reference to Skill and Purpose

The phrases and words in each category can frequently be interchanged. Look at the sample essays, and pay attention to the context in which the phrases and words are used. You will get a good idea of when and how to use them.

Speaking 1 (S1)   To Hesitate (to give yourself more time to think)

■ **Let's see**
■ **That's an interesting/a good question**
■ **Let me think**
■ **That's a good question**

Speaking 2 (S2)   To Give an Opinion

■ **(Why) I believe**
■ **I'd like to explain why**

- **Personally**
- **I'd enjoy**
- **I would prefer/be**
- **I think**
- **In my opinion**
- **As far as I'm concerned**
- **It seems to me**
- **I'd/He feel/feels**

Speaking 3 (S3)   To Set Up a Condition

- **If**
- **Even if**
- **If I could**
- **Whether (or not) to**
- **. . . as though**

Speaking 4 (S4)   To Further the Argument

- **First (of all) . . . Second . . . Third**
- **In addition**
- **There are (three) reasons why**
- **Similarly**
- **Furthermore**
- **Moreover**
- **Further**
- **As an example**
- **For instance**

➡

- What's more
- . . . a good idea
- . . . in favor of

Speaking 5 (S5)   To Summarize/Conclude

- In conclusion
- Finally
- As a result
- In summary
- Therefore
- To sum up
- In other words
- To summarize
- Then
- In brief
- On the whole
- To conclude
- As we have seen,
- As has been said,
- Thereby
- Most importantly

Speaking 6 (S6)   To Show Ability

- (I'd be) able to
- I can/could
- I'm able to

- I'd be capable of
- . . . enables

Speaking 7 (S7)   To Show Cause/Reason and Effect/Result

- As a result
- Consequently
- Because (of)
- Due to
- Thanks to
- If this occurs, then
- To this end
- Since
- For this reason

Speaking 8 (S8)   To Show Time Relationships

- Immediately
- Then
- Later
- Afterwards
- After
- Before
- While
- During
- As soon as
- As

- **Sometimes**
- **When**
- **Ever/Never**
- **Every day/month/year**

Speaking 9 (S9)   To Generalize

- **Overall**
- **For the most part**
- **In general**
- **Generally speaking**
- **By and large**

Speaking 10 (S10)   To Show Contrast

- **Some may argue that**
- **Although**
- **Even though**
- **Whereas**
- **While**
- **Instead**
- **In contrast**
- **On the one hand**
- **On the other hand**
- **However**
- **In spite of**
- **Despite**

- Unlike
- On the contrary
- But
- Neither/nor
- . . . rather than
- . . . mistakenly
- Curiously
- Not until
- Surprisingly

Speaking 11 (S11)   To Show Emphasis

- Above all
- Obviously
- Clearly
- Evidently
- Actually
- In fact
- Certainly
- Definitely
- Extremely
- Indeed
- Absolutely
- Positively
- Unquestionably
- Without a doubt

Speaking 12 (S12)   To State Policy

- The policy is (that)
- The policy states

Speaking 13 (S13)   To Argue a Point/Make a Suggestion

- . . . seems to warrant
- . . . contends
- . . . argues
- . . . justifies
- This observation is supported by
- . . . to plead
- . . . suggests
- The suggestion is valid
- . . . proposes
- Both . . . and
- Also
- . . . claims
- . . . states
- The suggestion is
- Not only . . . but also
- There are benefits

Speaking 14 (S14)   To Show Disagreement

- . . . objects (to)
- . . . disagrees with

- . . . opposes
- . . . contradicts
- . . . are invalid
- Others may argue

Speaking 15 (S15) To Choose one Option Over Another

- . . . might be/is the better option
- . . . makes it a better policy
- . . . is the better alternative

Speaking 16 (S16) To Show Similarity

- Just as
- As . . . as
- In the same way
- Similarly
- Likewise
- As in/as with/as was/etc.
- Like

Speaking 17 (S17) To Show Purpose

- In order to
- For
- So that
- So as to
- . . . compensation for

Speaking 18 (S18)   To Show Evidence/Give an Example

- **As evidence of**
- **The legitimacy of**
- **Such as**
- **For example**
- **A few of these are**
- **In the case of**
- **In addition (to)**
- **For one thing . . . for another**

Speaking 19 (S19)   To State the Problem

- **The problem is (how)**

Speaking 20 (S20)   To State the Options

- **She is considering two (various) options**
- **One option is**
- **The other option is**
- **. . . might/may be an/the easier /better option**
- **. . . has (two) alternatives**

Chapter 3 Speaking Skill Development

A. Websites for Improving Listening Skills

In the TOEFL speaking section, you will hear only the speakers; you will not see them. To improve your listening/speaking skills, try every day to listen to native English speakers. Listening to the radio or the computer is better than watching television because when you watch television you can look at the speakers' lips. You will not see the speakers during the administration of the TOEFL. Although watching television, especially with closed captions, is beneficial, try to use the radio and computer frequently.

Below is a list of academic lecture and English learning Websites that you will find helpful. These sites will help you practice listening to the types of academic and campus-based lectures you will hear on the test. In addition, the pronunciation sites will help you improve your speaking ability.

- http://tesl-ej.org/ej17/m3.html (including ten sites)
- www.eslhome.com/esl/listen
- www.stanford.edu/~efs/tesol03listening

- www.public.iastate.edu/~hschmidt/listeninglinks.htm
- www.cdlponline.org
- www.esl.about.com/cs/listening
- www.esl-lab.com
- www.englishbaby.com
- www.en.wikipeida.org/wiki/marketplace_%28radio_program%29

Part III

The Writing Section

Chapter 4 Description of Tasks

In the writing section you will type two essays into the computer. The first essay is called the *independent task*. You will have 30 minutes to prepare, write, and revise a minimum of 300 words on an essay topic from personal experience, not from given material (a reading passage and lecture). The second essay is called the *integrated task*. You will first read a 250–300 word passage in three minutes and then hear a 230–300-word lecture on the same topic that is approximately two minutes long. The information is related, but it does not repeat. You will take notes on the information in each part, and then you will have 20 minutes to prepare, write, and revise a 150–225-word response about how the information is related. In contrast to the independent task, the integrated task does *not* ask for your opinion.

A. The Independent Task

In almost all the independent tasks, you will be asked to compare how two thoughts, ideas, or proposals are similar or how they are different. You can do either or both. You will need to choose which idea you agree with or which one you think is better. Your prompt will be something that asks you to look at two sides of an argument.

1. Sample Prompt with Response

> **Many people have pets. Other people don't. In your opinion, is it a good idea to have a pet, such as a bird, dog, or cat? Why or why not? Use specific reasons and examples to support your answer.**

30 minutes to organize, write, and edit your essay. On average, an effective essay will be at least 300 words.

Preparation Notes

Divide your time between brainstorming (writing down ideas quickly), writing, and editing. A good suggestion is 5 minutes for brainstorming, 20 minutes for writing, and 5 minutes for editing.

*Even if the prompt does not actually say "**Why or why not?"** **use specific reasons and examples to support your answer**, making sure you defend your arguments with personal examples. Maybe you don't have an opinion about the question, so before you begin the essay, brainstorm some pros and cons:*

Description of Tasks

<u>*For*</u>

- *Companionship*
- *Reduces stress*
- *Protection*
- *Exercise*

<u>*Against*</u>

- *Dirty/smelly*
- *Expensive*
- *Have to be around for them*

If you brainstorm first, you won't have to be thinking of specific examples while you write.

- ***Here is a sample response. <u>Underlined</u> words and phrases are categorized in Chapter 5, Phrases and Vocabulary for the Writing Section with Reference to Skill and Purpose.***

Many people in the world have pets, and <u>there are different reasons why</u> **(W1)** people do. <u>Some</u> **(W10)** of these pets are treated like actual family members. <u>Other</u> **(W10)** people who do not own pets cannot understand why some people have pets and treat them as they do. <u>Although</u> **(W10)** some people think it's not a good idea to have a pet, <u>I believe</u> **(W2)** it's <u>beneficial</u> **(W15)**. People who don't have pets <u>may</u> **(W3)** think that pets are dirty. <u>If</u> **(W3)** you have a dog, you have to clean up animal hair or accidents they have. <u>Moreover</u> **(W4)**, there's <u>often</u> **(W8)** a smell in the apartment from the pet. <u>In addition</u> **(W4)**,

➡

---

buying the pet food and supplies and paying for visits to the veterinarian <u>can be</u> (**W3**) very expensive. One has to be <u>frequently</u> (**W8**) around <u>either</u> (**W10**) to walk the pet <u>or</u> (**W10**) simply feed it. <u>On the other hand</u> (**W10**), <u>there are many positive reasons for</u> (**W1**) owning a pet. An animal, <u>such as</u> (**W18**) a dog or cat, can keep you company. <u>Furthermore</u> (**W4**), the pet is always happy to see you <u>when</u> (**W8**) you come home. One can get exercise, <u>for example</u> (**W18**), by taking it on a walk. <u>As a result</u> (**W5**) of patting it, one can relax. <u>Sometimes</u> (**W8**) a person can get a dog <u>so that</u> (**W17**) she can feel safe <u>due to</u> (**W7**) its bark or simply its presence. I didn't have a dog growing up, and <u>once</u> (**W8**) I got one, I was surprised at how quickly she became a beloved part of our family, <u>in fact</u> (**W11**), enabling us all to share in her well-being and happiness.

<u>In conclusion</u> (**W5**), there are people who think pets are a nuisance <u>because of</u> (**W7**) <u>both</u> (**W4**) their smell <u>and</u> (**W4**) the mess they create. <u>Also</u> (**W4**), pets are demanding of time and can be quite costly. <u>In contrast</u> (**W10**), those people who have pets know what a welcome addition they can be to any person or family. <u>Clearly</u> (**W11**), they bring companionship and love. <u>What's more</u> (**W4**), their need for exercise can help anyone become more active. <u>For the most part</u> (**W9**), their presence can reduce stress. <u>Therefore</u> (**W5**), <u>I suggest that</u> (**W2**) having a pet is <u>better than</u> (**W15**) not having one.

2. Sample Prompt with Response

> **Some people think that the best place to raise children is in a city. Others think that the best place is in the countryside. Compare these two views. Which view do you agree with? Explain why.**

30 minutes to organize, write, and edit your essay. On average, an effective essay will be at least 300 words.

Preparation Notes

Divide your time between brainstorming (writing down ideas quickly), writing, and editing. A good suggestion is 5 minutes for brainstorming, 20 minutes for writing, and 5 minutes for editing.

*Even if the prompt does not actually say "**Why or why not?**" **use specific reasons and examples to support your answer,** making sure you defend your arguments with personal examples. Maybe you don't have an opinion about the question, so before you begin the essay, brainstorm some pros and cons:*

City	*Countryside*
▪ *Experiences*	▪ *Cleaner*
▪ *Variety of people*	▪ *Less pressure*
▪ *Fosters independence*	▪ *Closer to nature*
▪ *Closer to playmates*	

59

If you brainstorm first, you won't have to be thinking of specific examples while you write.

■ *Here is a sample response. <u>Underlined</u> words and phrases are categorized in Chapter 5, Phrases and Vocabulary for the Writing Section with Reference to Skill and Purpose.*

<u>As soon as</u> (**W8**) the decision is made to have children, parents debate <u>whether</u> (**W3**) <u>it is better</u> (**W15**) to raise them in the city <u>or</u> (**W3**) in the countryside. <u>Although</u> (**W10**) <u>sometimes</u> (**W8**) a job may dictate where to raise a family, <u>if I had the choice</u> (**W13**), <u>I'd prefer</u> (**W2**) to raise my children in a city.

<u>Objectively</u> (**W11**), <u>there are some benefits to</u> (**W1**) raising children in the countryside. <u>First</u> (**W4**), there is less pollution. <u>Second</u> (**W4**), there are fewer social pressures. <u>As a result</u> (**W5**), children don't have to grow up so quickly. <u>On the whole</u> (**W5**), <u>some may argue that</u> (**W10**) one can feel closer to <u>as well as</u> (**W16**) appreciate nature living in the countryside.

<u>On the other hand</u> (**W10**), <u>there are more benefits</u> (**W1**) to living in a city. City children are exposed to more culture. <u>In addition</u> (**W4**), there is a greater variety of types of people children can be exposed to, expanding their

horizons. <u>Furthermore</u> **(W4)**, living in a city can foster more independence as children can get around by themselves on public transportation and not depend on their parents. <u>Finally</u> **(W5)**, children can live closer to friends and have more opportunities for interaction. I was raised in the countryside, and <u>although</u> **(W10)** I do appreciate the beauty of nature, I was <u>oftentimes</u> **(W8)** bored as a child and had very few friends living nearby to play with. I hope to raise my own children in a city <u>so that</u> **(W17)** they can <u>frequently</u> **(W8)** visit museums and the theater and attend concerts. <u>As far as I'm concerned</u> **(W2)**, the types of people living in the countryside are very similar. <u>In other words</u> **(W5)**, I hope to expose my own children to an array of people: rich and poor, old and young, differing social classes, etc.

    <u>To sum up</u> **(W5)**, <u>whereas</u> **(W10)** <u>there are some benefits to</u> **(W1)** living in the countryside, <u>namely</u> **(W6)** a healthier environment and fewer temptations, the richness of city life, <u>coupled with</u> **(W4)** the array of opportunities and ease of mobility, make living in the city a <u>better option for me</u> **(W15)**.

B. The Integrated Task

In all the integrated tasks, you will read a short passage and then listen to a talk on the same subject. You should take notes while you read and while you listen. You will then be asked to write about the difference between what you read and what you heard. Although what you hear and what you read will be about the same topic, the information on each will differ. In other words, what you hear will contradict what you read. You will not give your opinion. While you write, you can look at your notes and at the reading passage.

1. Sample Prompt with Essay

Read a sample reading passage in three minutes.

There is a small but growing movement in the United States and around the world against immunizing, that is, giving shots to babies and children. Those who choose not to vaccinate their children argue that the medical profession provides one-sided and dangerous propaganda in pediatric offices and at health-care facilities. They believe that natural immunity is better and that babies at two months of age are too young to receive an assault on their immune system.

First, those in the movement cite anecdotal evidence that those children who are vaccinated against once-common childhood diseases, such as measles, mumps, polio, and whooping cough, are more likely to suffer from chronic ear infections as well as from consistent, low-grade infections. They contend that acquiring childhood diseases naturally actually benefits the immune system, whereas they have heard of children and adults who have contacted other diseases and disabilities as a result of being immunized.

In addition, they argue that children can still get the disease for which they were vaccinated. They report that among reported measles cases, the overwhelming majority were among those who were fully vaccinated. They suggest preventing disease through natural healing. Rather than injecting young bodies with toxic substances and foreign proteins and viruses—the substances contained in vaccines—they claim that cleansing bodies periodically of toxins can keep bodies free of bacteria and viruses. Changing poor lifestyle habits, those in the movement contend, is a better means of eradicating childhood diseases than is immunization.

Furthermore, they assert that the vaccines themselves are inherently dangerous, whether or not they prevent disease. In support of this argument, they point to lethal additives in many vaccines and the fact that vaccines are tested on animals, not on humans.

Preparation Notes

Three minutes to read and take notes is not a long time. Because the passage is quite difficult, try to understand the main arguments. You can use abbreviations to save time. Perhaps this paragraph could come after Preparation Notes?

- **In the three minutes you have to read the passage, you could write down:**
- *Group against giving shots to babs. & child.*
- *Those w/ shots get other diseases—better to get childhd. dis.*
- *Get dis vac. agst.*
- *Vac. themselves are dang. Tested on anim. not hums.*

Now listen to a lecture on the topic you just read about while you take notes:

Professor: Recently those who challenge the practice of vaccinating babies and children seemingly provide compelling arguments. First, they state that natural immunity is better. But in Australia alone there were 581 deaths from diseases preventable by immunizations between 1989 and 1998. OK. Next, the U.S. Food and Drug Administration refutes the assertion that diseases and disabilities are spread through immunizations. Despite millions of doses of vaccine being administered worldwide, no substantiated cases of actual disease or disability has been documented. In Germany a study of 496 vaccinated and unvaccinated children found that those who had received inoculations in the first three months of life had fewer infections overall than the unvaccinated group. It is far too easy, the administration affirms, to attribute the increasing numbers of asthma or autism cases to inoculations rather than to investigate further. Another faulty assumption is that those vaccinated actually develop the disease. Last year, fewer than 10 percent of those being vaccinated against measles actually fell sick, and none of them died. Next, the proposal that natural healing, or cleansing, is superior to immunization is absurd. No homeopathic alternative to immunization has been successful, and to suggest that the world is in a position to "change poor lifestyle habits" any time soon is unrealistic. And their final claim that vaccines themselves are dangerous is untruthful. The exact opposite is true. Even though vaccines can cause side effects, such as pain, redness, or tenderness, no one has died from a hepatitis B vaccine. Unfortunately, every year 5,000 unvaccinated people die from hepatitis B. So while some children develop mild symptoms of the disease after being vaccinated, the substantial number of deaths in areas of the world without vaccinations certainly negates any argument for ceasing immunization.

Preparation Notes

- ▪ *While listening, you could write down:*
- ▪ *Challenged each point in reading*
- ▪ *Nonimmuniz. Do die*
- ▪ *No deaths w/immun.*
- ▪ *No cases of nat. healing*
- ▪ *Immunz. actually not harmful*

Narrator: Summarize the points made in the lecture, being sure to specifically explain how they cast doubt on points made in the reading passage.

---

20 minutes to organize, write, and edit your essay. On average, an effective essay will be 150 to 225 words.

- ▪ *Here is a sample response. <u>Underlined</u> words and phrases are categorized in Chapter 5, Phrases and Vocabulary for the Writing Section with Reference to Skill and Purpose.*

The lecturer <u>contends</u> (**W13**) that the arguments made by the anti-immunization movement are <u>invalid</u> (**W4**). <u>Even though</u> (**W10**) the movement <u>seems to offer strong arguments against</u> (**W15**) vaccinating babies and children, <u>these arguments, one by one, can be challenged</u> (**W14**).

First (**W4**), they <u>state</u> (**W13**) that natural immunity is preferable; <u>however</u> (**W10**), those not immunized in the world have died. <u>Second</u> (**W4**), the group <u>claims</u> (**W13**) that diseases are contracted by immunizations, <u>yet</u> (**W10**) no such cases have been found. It's easier to say that a rise in certain diseases or conditions is due to immunizations <u>rather than</u> (**W10**) bothering to investigate further. <u>Third</u> (**W4**), the argument that natural healing is better than immunizations is <u>absurd</u> (**W14**). <u>In fact</u> (**W11**), no such healing has been proven successful. <u>Finally</u> (**W5**), <u>the assertion</u> (**W15**) that the vaccine itself is harmful <u>is false</u> (**W15**). Vaccinations <u>may</u> (**W3**) cause pain; <u>however</u> (**W10**), no one has ever died from a shot.

<u>To summarize</u> (**W5**), the great number of deaths in areas of the world without vaccinations is <u>clearly proof enough</u> (**W13**) that the movement against immunizations is <u>not to be taken seriously</u> (**W14**). <u>In other words</u> (**W6**), the claims of this movement <u>have no scientific basis</u> (**W14**).

2. Sample Prompt with Essay

Read a sample reading passage in three minutes:

One of the most enduring mysteries of modern times, the Bermuda Triangle, has fascinated the world for decades. Is it really true that the 440,000-square-mile triangle, whose three corners touch Florida, Bermuda, and Puerto Rico, literally swallows ships and aircraft? Does it really have mystical properties?

The first reports of strange phenomena in this area of the southwestern Atlantic date as far back as 1492 when Christopher Columbus sailed into the area. Columbus's journal entry dated October 11, 1492, contains an account of a malfunctioning compass and the presence of strange lights in the sky, including a "a great flame of fire" which crashed into the ocean.

Stories of more than just a single death while sailing through the triangle have believers. In its day, the 1872 disappearance of the crew of the famous ship the *Mary Celeste* was notorious. The lost ship was eventually found, but its entire crew was missing. Because for so many years no explanation could be found for the crew's abandonment, many have proposed that the sailors died while sailing through the triangle.

The most compelling tale of mysterious happenings in the Bermuda Triangle centers around the disappearance of six U.S. military aircraft in 1945 as they were flying through the region.

A squadron of five bombers on a routine training mission was lost. The sixth plane, a search plane was lost as well.

Preparation Notes

Three minutes to read and take notes is not a long time. Because the passage contains many details, try to write down the main points. You can use abbreviations to save time.

- *In the 3 minutes you have to read the passage, you could write down:*
- *Berm. 444,000 miles*
- *C. Columbus fire in sky*
- *1872 Mary Celeste crew*
- *1945 6 US aircraft*

Now listen to a lecture on the topic you just read about while you take notes:

Professor: Looking at some of the most famous incidents attributed to the Bermuda Triangle, also known as the Devil's Triangle, historical researchers and scientists have found that the mysteries of the Bermuda Triangle, so named in 1964, are more fiction than fact.

Let's start with the Christopher Columbus report. Although the "great flame of fire" report sounds too incredible to have happened, such an event can be scientifically explained. First, the compass malfunction was probably the result of the discrepancy between true north and magnetic north. Second, the lights that appeared to be in the sky were actually reflections of land lights. Finally, the "great flame of fire" may well have been a meteor falling into the sea.

Sudden unexpected storms or downward air currents provide strong scientific evidence for previously unexplained phenomena. In addition, many maritime disasters attributed to the Bermuda Triangle didn't occur anywhere near the area. The most exaggerated of these tales is that of the lost ship the *Mary Celeste*, which went off course in 1872, and was eventually found near the coast of Portugal.

Many maritime disasters and disappearances have been attributed to the Bermuda Triangle. Take the case of the six missing U.S. military aircraft in 1945. This incident has a less than mysterious explanation. The squadron most likely went off course as result of malfunctioning navigational equipment, poor weather, inexperienced pilots, and a squadron commander who was unfit to fly. Once the squadron commander became disoriented, he may have led the squadron north and east instead of south and west, which explains why no wreckage was ever found. If the planes ran out of fuel past the continental shelf of the Atlantic, the planes could have sunk to a depth of 30,000 feet below the surface of the ocean. As for the search plane, an examination of naval records shows that the plane exploded about 20 seconds after taking off. In other words, the plane never made it into the area known as the Bermuda Triangle. It seems that none of the aircraft disappeared as a result of mysterious phenomena.

Preparation Notes

- ***While listening, you could write down:***
- *Challenged each point in reading, no mys.*
  All scien. expls.
- *CC: compass malfunction, light-meteor*
- *Mary Celeste-off Portugal, not in area*
- *1945 5 US planes off course, 6th exploded on takeoff*

Narrator: Summarize the points made in the lecture, being sure to specifically explain how they cast doubt on points made in the reading passage.

---

20 minutes to organize, write, and edit your essay. On average, an effective essay will be 150 to 225 words.

- ***Here is a sample response. <u>Underlined</u> words and phrases are categorized in Chapter 5, Phrases and Vocabulary for the Writing Section with Reference to Skill and Purpose.***

Although **(W10)** the world has been fascinated for many years with mysterious disappearances and occurrences in the area known as the Bermuda Triangle, the professor scientifically disputes **(W14)** several of the most famous cases, claiming that **(W13)** none **(W10)** have any scientific basis **(W14)**.

First **(W4)**, he examines **(W13)** the case of Christopher Columbus's nonworking compass and the great ball of fire. The professor asserts **(W13)** that the confusion with the compass was due to **(W7)** confusion between true and magnetic north. Furthermore **(W4)**, he proposes **(W13)** that the great ball of fire was a meteor.

Second **(W4)**, the famous shipwreck of the Mary Celeste in 1872 did not take place anywhere near the Triangle. Surprisingly **(W11)**, the ship was discovered near Portugal.

Third **(W4)**, the most recent case, that of the six missing U.S. aircraft in 1945, has no scientific basis **(W14)**. Five planes and the search plane were all reported missing in the area. There are several explanations for **(W1)** the disappearances. The planes may have had both **(W4)** bad weather and **(W4)** inexperienced pilots. The lead pilot could have led the group off course. In fact **(W11)**, none **(W10)** of the planes was found in the area. Actually **(W11)**, the search plane exploded immediately after **(W8)** takeoff.

To conclude (**W5**), the cases that seem to support the mystery of the Bermuda Triangle, one by one, can be challenged (**W14**). The professor offers (**W15**) arguments (**W15**) contradicting (**W14**) supposed disappearances and occurrences caused by (**W7**) ships and aircraft being in the Triangle.

Chapter 5 Phrases and Vocabulary for the Writing Section with Reference to Skill and Purpose

The phrases and words in each category can frequently be interchanged. Look at the sample essays, and pay attention to the context in which the phrases and words are used. You will get a good idea of when and how to use them.

Writing 1 (W1)   To State the Reasons

- **There are different reasons why**
- **There are several explanations for**
- **There are many positive/negative reasons for**
- **There are some/more/fewer benefits/disadvantages to**

Writing 2 (W2)   To Give an Opinion

- **(Why) I believe**
- **I'd like to explain why**

- **Personally**
- **I'd enjoy**
- **I would prefer**
- **I think**
- **In my opinion**
- **As far as I'm concerned**
- **It seems to me**
- **I suggest**

Writing 3 (W3)　　To Set Up a Condition

- **If**
- **Even if**
- **If I could**
- **Whether (or not)**
- **. . . may/might**
- **. . . can be**

Writing 4 (W4)　　To Further the Argument

- **First (of all) . . . Second . . . Third**
- **In addition**
- **There are three reasons why**
- **Similarly**
- **Furthermore**
- **Moreover**
- **Further**
- **As an example**

- **For instance**
- **What's more**
- **Not only . . . but also**
- **. . . including**
- **More than**
- **Also**
- **. . . coupled with**
- **Both . . . and**

Writing 5 (W5)   To Summarize/Conclude

- **In conclusion**
- **Finally**
- **As a result (of)**
- **In summary**
- **Therefore**
- **To sum up**
- **In other words**
- **To summarize**
- **Then**
- **In brief**
- **On the whole**
- **To conclude**
- **As we have seen**
- **As has been said**

Writing 6 (W6)   To Restate or Repeat an Argument

- To put it differently
- To repeat
- Namely
- That is
- In other words

Writing 7 (W7)   To Show Cause/Reason and Effect/Result

- Consequently
- Because (of)
- Due to
- Thanks to
- If this occurs, then
- To this end
- Since
- For this reason
- As a result
- Caused by

Writing 8 (W8)   To Show Time Relationships

- Immediately
- Then
- Later
- Afterwards
- After

- Before
- While
- During
- As soon as
- As
- Sometimes
- Last
- Frequently
- When
- Once
- Often
- Oftentimes

Writing 9 (W9)   To Generalize

- Overall
- For the most part
- In general
- Generally speaking
- By and large

Writing 10 (W10)   To Show Contrast/Make an Exception

- Some may argue that
- Although
- Even though
- Whereas

- Instead
- In contrast
- On the one hand
- On the other hand
- However
- In spite of
- Despite
- Unlike
- On the contrary
- But
- Yet
- Rather than
- Either
- Or
- Nor
- Neither
- Either . . . or
- Neither . . . nor
- Nevertheless
- Nonetheless
- Sometimes
- Once in a while
- Occasionally
- Some...other(s)
- Other(s)
- Often
- None

Writing 11 (W11)   To Emphasize

- Above all
- Obviously
- Clearly
- Evidently
- Actually
- In fact
- Certainly
- Definitely
- Extremely
- Indeed
- Absolutely
- Positively
- Surprisingly
- Unquestionably
- Without a doubt
- Objectively
- In fact

Writing 12 (W12)   To State Policy

- The policy is (that)

Writing 13 (W13)   To Argue/Make a Suggestion

- . . . seems to warrant
- . . . contend/s

➡

- . . . argue/s
- . . . justify/ies
- This observation is supported by
- To plead
- . . . suggest/s
- The suggestion is valid
- . . . propose/s
- . . . claim/s
- . . . state/s
- . . . clearly proof enough
- If I had the choice
- . . . examine/s
- . . . assert/s

Writing 14 (W14) To Show Disagreement

- . . . object/s (to)
- . . . disagree/s with
- . . . contradict/s
- . . . doesn't/don't support
- . . . is/are invalid
- These arguments, one by one, can be challenged
- . . . is absurd/ridiculous/unfounded/illogical
- . . . not to be taken seriously
- . . . has/have no scientific basis
- . . . dispute/s

Writing 15 (W15)   To Choose One Option over Another

- . . . might be the better option
- . . . make/s it a better policy
- It's beneficial/better/positive
- It's detrimental/worse/negative
- . . . is true/false
- The assertion that. . .
- . . . seem/s to offer strong arguments for/against
- . . . is/are better/worse than

Writing 16 (W16)   To Show Similarity

- Just as
- As . . . as
- In the same way
- Similarly
- Likewise
- As in/as with/as was/etc.

Writing 17 (W17)   To Show Purpose

- In order to
- For
- So that
- So as to

Writing 18 (W18)   To Show Evidence/Give an Example

- **As evidence of**
- **The legitimacy of**
- **Such as**
- **For example**
- **A few of these are**
- **In the case of**
- **In addition**
- **For one thing . . . for another**

Writing 19 (W19)   To State the Problem

- **The problem is (how)**
- **The question is**
- **What is being asked/challenged**

Writing 20 (W20)   To State the Options

- **One option is**
- **The other option is**

Chapter 6 Writing Skill Development

A. Suggestions for the Independent Task

Every day set aside a half an hour to write an essay. You will notice two things: (1) You will be able to write more and more each day. (2) The types of tasks in the Independent Task section tend to be very similar. Below you will find 10 examples of the kinds of tasks that you will find on the test. Although you will not be asked something identical, what you will be asked will be very similar in design. You should be able to make up some by yourself for practice.

- Some people prefer to live with a roommate. Others prefer to live alone. Compare the advantages of each choice. Which of these two options do you prefer? Use specific reasons to support your answer.

- The government has decided to build a new airport. Some people think that *your* community would be a good place to locate the airport. Compare the advantages and disadvantages of establishing a new airport in your community. Use specific details in your response.

- Do you agree or disagree with the following statement? Children should help with tasks around the house from a very young age. Use specific reasons and examples to support your position.

- People act differently when they wear different clothes. Do you agree that different clothes can change the way people behave? Use specific examples to support your answer.

- Some people believe that playing games can teach us about life. Do you agree? Why or why not? Use specific examples and reasons to support your answer.

- Some colleges and universities allow students to declare their majors only after their sophomore year. Some universities make students declare their majors in the first year. Which policy do you think is better and why?

- Some colleges and universities require students to complete a certain number of hours of community service in order to graduate. Do you think this is a good policy? Why or why not? Use specific reasons and examples.

- Some colleges and universities require students to live on campus all four years. Do you think this is a good policy? Why or why not? Use specific reasons and examples.

- Some professors at colleges and universities give open-book exams. Others do not. Which practice do you think is better and why? Use specific reasons.

- Some cities think that a way to limit pollution and congestion is to tax drivers heavily who drive into the city each day but who live elsewhere. What do you think about this policy? Do you support it? Why or why not? Use specific reasons.

B. Suggestions for the Integrated Task

Because in the integrated task you will read and listen to a lecture on a topic and then write about it, this task is much more difficult than the independent task. The listening sites with academic lectures listed in Chapter 3 are an excellent place to begin. In addition, study the phrases and vocabulary you will need to use to compare and contrast because what you read and what you hear will always contradict each other. Try to find topics you are studying or that are in the news that seem to contradict one another, for example, the debate about whether global warming is a real threat or not. Once you identify such a topic, find articles on both sides of the issue and then write a 20-minute comparison/contrast essay.

Part IV

Vocabulary Development

Chapter 7 Summarizing Practice

A. Increasing Vocabulary through Reading

Every day find an article of approximately 250 words. Look in magazines or find an article from a newspaper on the Web or in a library. Read the article through and highlight five words you do not know. The words you highlight should be important to the understanding of the article. Look them up and make sure that the meaning you find in the dictionary is the correct meaning as it relates to the article. Keep these words in your own dictionary and review them frequently.

B. Increasing Vocabulary with the Academic Word Lists

Analyses of academic discussions and lectures have determined which words lecturers use most often. The most frequently used words appear below in five lists which were compiled by Averil Coxhead of Massey University in Palmerston North, New Zealand. Sublist 1 contains the words most frequently heard in lectures, followed by Sublist 2, and so on. The words on these lists may or may not appear on your TOEFL exam. They appear here because these words are important for your academic studies, and you should be familiar with many of them and attempt to incorporate them into your writing and speaking. According to Coxhead, "The more words students know well and can use, the more meaning they can communicate in a wide variety of circumstances" (*Essentials of Teaching Academic Vocabulary*, p.1. Houghton Mifflin Company, USA (Boston and New York), 2006). Enter "Academic Word List" on Google, and you will find many helpful sites and exercises using the Academic Word List.

Here is my suggestion: Highlight the words you do know. Start with Sublist 1. Make file cards with the word on the front, the part of speech, the meaning, and the word in a sentence on the back. Feel free to translate the word. Sometimes there is more than one meaning to a word. Write down the most commonly used meanings.

Review the words frequently: on the bus, in your room, between classes, *anywhere!*

Look for them in the articles you read (see Increasing Vocabulary through Listening directly above), and listen for them on the suggested Websites (see Chapter 3) in the listening section. Try to use these words frequently when you speak and when you write.

Make File Cards for the Words You Don't Know

Prepare file cards for words you don't know. For example, from Sublist 1: write the word **ENVIRONMENT** on one side of the card. On the other side write the following: *1. Part of Speech: Noun 2. Meaning: The surrounding conditions 3. Sentence: Many* *people today are worried about the* environment *because of global warming and pollution.* **4. Translation** = *Write the meaning of "environment" in your native language.*

Sublist 1 of the Academic Word List

This sublist contains the most frequently used words.

analysis	established	occur
approach	estimate	percent
area	evidence	period
assessment	export	policy
assume	factors	principle
authority	financial	procedure
available	formula	process
benefit	function	required
concept	identified	research
consistent	income	response
constitutional	indicate	role
context	individual	section
contract	interpretation	sector
create	involved	significant
data	issues	similar
definition	labor	source
derived	legal	specific
distribution	legislation	structure
economic	major	theory
environment	method	variables

Sublist 2 of Academic Word List

This sublist contains the next 60 most frequently used words.

achieve	design	potential
acquisition	distinction	previous
administration	elements	primary
affect	equation	purchase
appropriate	evaluation	range
aspects	features	region
assistance	final	regulations
categories	focus	relevant
chapter	impact	resident
commission	injury	resources
community	institute	restricted
complex	investment	security
computer	items	sought
conclusion	journal	select
conduct	maintenance	site
consequences	normal	strategies
construction	obtained	survey
consumer	participation	text
credit	perceived	traditional
cultural	positive	transfer

Sublist 3 of Academic Word List

This sublist contains the third most frequently used words.

alternative	emphasis	philosophy
circumstances	ensure	physical
comments	excluded	proportion
compensation	framework	published
components	funds	reaction
consent	illustrated	registered
considerable	immigration	reliance
constant	implies	removed
constraints	initial	scheme
contribution	instance	sequence
convention	interaction	sex
coordination	justification	shift
core	layer	specified
corporate	link	sufficient
corresponding	location	task
criteria	maximum	technical
deduction	minorities	techniques
demonstrate	negative	technology
document	outcomes	validity
dominant	partnership	volume

Sublist 4 of Academic Word List

This sublist contains the next 60 most frequently used words.

access	error	parallel
adequate	ethnic	parameters
annual	goals	phase
apparent	granted	predicted
approximated	hence	principal
attitudes	hypothesis	prior
attributed	implementation	professional
civil	implications	project
code	imposed	promote
commitment	integration	regime
communication	internal	resolution
concentration	investigation	restrained
conference	job	series
contrast	label	statistics
cycle	mechanism	status
debate	obvious	stress
despite	occupational	subsequent
dimensions	option	sum
domestic	output	summary
emerged	overall	undertaken

Sublist 5 of Academic Word List

This sublist contains the next 60 most frequently used words.

academic	evolution	orientation
adjustment	expansion	perspective
alter	exposure	precise
amendment	external	prime
aware	facilitate	psychology
capacity	fundamental	pursue
challenge	generated	ratio
clause	generation	rejected
compounds	image	revenue
conflict	liberal	stability
consultation	license	styles
contact	logic	substitution
decline	marginal	sustainable
discretion	medical	symbolic
draft	mental	target
enable	modified	transition
energy	monitoring	trend
enforcement	network	version
entities	notion	welfare
equivalent	objective	whereas

Appendix 1 Grammar

A. Grammar Pretest

Correct all the errors in the following sentences. The errors focus on the topics covered in the this appendix: sentence fragments, run-on sentences, parallelism, subject-verb agreement, pronouns, who/whom, sentence variety, and dangling/misplaced modifiers. If the sentence is CORRECT, write C.

1. Crying during her acceptance speech, the best actress award was presented to Nicole Kidman.

2. I don't want to be an architect because I don't like it.

3. After I came to America.

4. I studied all night for the midterm, I'm sure I got an A.

5. A janitor's salary is higher than a teacher.

6. Neither the students nor I are going to the reception.

7. Collecting seashells are my hobby.

8. Me and my brother are majoring in sports management.

9. Return the library book to whomever is at the reception desk.

10. I moved into an apartment. I threw out all my old notebooks. I bought some new furniture.

11. I only read half the assignment.

12. Examining the sapphire, the jeweler discovered an imperfection.

13. Whom I know.

14. I always have and always will eat breakfast.

15. The population of Massachusetts is greater than Rhode Island.

16. My sister has been a nurse, actress, and designed stages.

17. Every sophomore, junior, and senior are required to update e-mail information.

18. A number of students in my English class is planning to complete an extra-credit project.

19. My roommate, she is planning to attend the summer session.

20. Who do you think will win the upcoming elections?

Corrections are in BOLD. The grammar rule that relates to the error and the rule number are marked. Some sentences may have more than one possible answer.

1. Crying during her acceptance speech, **Nicole Kidman accepted the best actress award.**

   Dangling/misplaced modifiers (8)

2. I don't want to be an architect because I don't like **architecture**.

   Pronouns (5)

3. After I came to America, **I learned English**.

   Sentence fragments (1)

4. I studied all night for the midterm**;** I'm sure I got an A.

   Run-on sentences (2)

5. A janitor's salary is higher than a teacher**'s**.

   Parallelism (3)

6. Neither the students nor I **am** going to the reception.

   Parallelism with paired conjunctions **(3)**

7. Collecting seashells **is** my hobby.

   Subject-verb agreement (4)

8. **My brother and I** are majoring in sports management.

   Pronouns (5)

9. Return the library book to **whoever** is at the reception desk.

   Who/whom (6)

10. **After moving** into an apartment, I **threw** out all my old notebooks **and** bought some new furniture.

    Sentence variety (7)

11. I **read only** half the assignment.

    Dangling/misplaced modifiers (8)

12. Examining the sapphire, the jeweler discovered an imperfection.

    Correct: Dangling/misplaced modifiers (8)

13. The boy whom I know is playing baseball.

    Sentence fragments (1)

14. I always have **eaten** and always will eat breakfast.

    Parallelism (3)

15. The population of Massachusetts is greater than Rhode Island**'s population.**

    Parallelism (3)

16. My sister has been a nurse, **an** actress, and **a stage designer.**

    Parallelism (3)

17. Every sophomore, junior, and senior **is** required to update his or her e-mail information.

    Subject-verb agreement (4)

18. A number of students in my English class **are** planning to complete an extra-credit project.

    Subject-verb agreement (4)

19. My roommate is planning to attend the summer session.

    Pronouns (5)

20. Who do you think will win the upcoming elections?

    Correct: Who/whom (6)

B.   Grammar Rules and Exercises

1. Sentence Fragments

- A **fragment** error is an incomplete sentence that does not express a complete thought. It may be missing a subject, a verb, or part of a subject or verb. It can also be a dependent clause that needs an independent clause.

Incorrect: Because I came to America.

The sentence should read, *Because I came to America,* **I met many Americans.** This dependent clause is *not* a sentence because it needs an independent clause to complete its meaning.

Incorrect: More students going to school.

The sentence should read, *More students* **are** *going to school.* The incorrect sentence contains an incomplete verb, which also creates a sentence fragment.

Incorrect: For me is very easy to understand people from Mississippi.

The sentence should read *For me* **it** *is very easy to understand people from Mississippi.* The incorrect sentence is missing a subject.

Incorrect: A class that is enjoyable.

The sentence should read, *A class that is enjoyable* **makes me interested in the subject.** This dependent clause is *not* a sentence because it needs a verb to complete its meaning.

2. Run-on Sentences

■ **A run-on** error is two or more sentences joined together without a word to connect them or a punctuation mark to separate them. If you put a comma between them, it is still incorrect. This error is called a *comma splice*.

Incorrect: Sometimes I like to be with one or two friends, sometimes I like to be with a large group of friends.

There are five ways to correct this run-on:

1. **Make two sentences.**

   Although your sentences will be grammatically correct, this is not the best way to solve the problem. It creates two choppy simple sentences instead of one complex one.

   Sometimes I like to be with one or two friends. Sometimes I like to be with a large group of friends.

2. **Use a coordinating conjunction (the word 'FANBOYS' can help you remember the coordinating conjunctions:** *for, and, nor, but, or, yet, so*).

   Sometimes I like to be with one or two friends, but sometimes I like to be with a large group of friends.

3. **Use a semicolon.** You can use a semicolon between two closely related sentences. Be careful not to overuse this punctuation mark.

   Sometimes I like to be with one or two friends; sometimes I like to be with a large group of friends.

4. **Use a transitional adverb (*however, therefore, consequently,* etc.).** Be careful of the punctuation in this construction. Subject + verb; **transitional adverb**, subject + verb.

   Sometimes I like to be with one or two friends; however; sometimes I like to be with a large group of friends.

5. **Make one of the clauses a dependent clause.**

   Although sometimes I like to be with one or two friends, sometimes I like to be with a large group of friends.

Run-on/Fragment Sentence Exercise 1

Label the following as sentences (S), fragments (F), or run-ons (RO). If sentences are F or RO, correct them.

_____ 1. For example, if you're going to buy a watch.

_____ 2. Learning English is not easy, it takes up your time and energy.

_____ 3. A good roommate who is quiet.

_____ 4. Getting out of the city for a camping trip.

_____ 5. My problem is the irregular verbs.

_____ 6. I spent three months looking for an apartment I couldn't find anything under $1,000 a month.

_____ 7. Twelve required courses in math and statistics.

_____ 8. What is your major?

_____ 9. A two-week vacation is a very short time to experience another country.

_____ 10. She couldn't understand the directions, she asked her friend for help.

Here are some possible fragment and run-on corrections for Exercise 1:

1.	F	… watch, go to a good jeweler.
2.	RO	… easy because it …
3.	F	… quiet is hard to find.
4.	F	… trip is a good idea.
5.	S	
6.	RO	… apartment, but I …
7.	F	There are twelve …
8.	S	
9.	S	
10.	R	… directions, so she …

Run-on/Fragment Sentence Exercise 2

From these sentences written by nonnative speakers, label the following as sentences (S), fragments (F), or run-ons (RO). If sentences are F or RO, correct them.

_____ 1. First who like to spend time with close friends can do many things in a short time.

_____ 2. I think children should be required to help with household tasks as soon as they are able to do so because parents can give their children some knowledge and include them as family members.

_____ 3. Second, when you are with a large number of friends.

_____ 4. Let me give an example, when I was in the first year of college, I always used to be with two of my friends.

_____ 5. Well, those are my basic points for wanting to go there, I hope that now you understand my desire.

_____ 6. I would probably choose Spain I think that this choice may create confusion with the readers, but I will give my reasons.

_____ 7. Regardless of gender, age, religion, and nationality, a teacher's role in learning is enormous because a teacher is a guide who will help open my eyes to some specific field which is totally unknown.

_____ 8. I prefer to have a teacher because if I learn by myself, maybe something mistake.

_____ 9. Sometimes when I have problems.

_____ 10. Two reasons.

_____ 11. Are teacher better computers?

_____ 12. When I was a child, I grew up in the countryside, I think it is a nice place for children's education.

_____ 13. When I saw a fire in the kitchen.

_____ 14. Through their personal experiences such as training.

_____ 15. If I don't have experience with it.

_____ 16. After having explained the advantages of having had a lifelong best friend and the disadvantages of going out with a diverse group of friends, I prefer to spend time with one or two close friends than with a large number of friends.

_____ 17. No matter what you think.

_____ 18. Even though unrelated to their occupation in the future.

_____ 19. Because I am a person who can feel nature beautifully, who helps other people, and who knows social rules.

_____ 20. However, sometimes I would like just to be with one or two of my friends rather than with a large number of friends.

Here are some possible fragment and run-on corrections to Exercise 2:

1.	F	First, people who	4. RO	example. When…
2.	S		5. RO	there. I hope
3.	F	friends, it is fun.	6. RO	Spain. I think

7. S

8. F   something is a mistake

9. F   problems, I call a friend.

10. F   There are two …

11. F   better than computers?

12. RO   countryside. I think …

13. F   kitchen, I screamed.

14. F   They learned a lot through…

15. F   it, I ask someone.

16. S

17. S

18. F   They took a summer job even though

19. F   beautifully, I help other people and know…

20. S

3.   Parallelism

- In writing, one must construct a sentence making sure its parts are parallel, or the sentence will be off balance. Always try to balance similar structures, especially in lists and series or around connecting words within your sentences. In order to make sure your writing is parallel, make sure you understand the following points:

   - Connect sentence parts with coordinating conjunctions.

   - A good clause or phrase combines the same kinds of words, phrases, or clauses. Combine a noun with a noun, not a noun with an adjective.

I.   Words

1.   noun + noun

   <u>Recession</u> or <u>inflation</u> will lead to disaster.

2. verb + verb

    The pharmacist <u>weighed</u> and <u>measured</u> the medicine.

3. adjective + adjective

    The child was <u>little</u>, yet surprisingly <u>strong</u>.

    With three or more items in a series, use commas.

    The play was <u>funny</u>, <u>enjoyable</u>, and <u>short</u>.

4. adverb + adverb

    He ran <u>quickly</u> but <u>carefully</u>.

II. **Phrases** (groups of words that lack either a subject or a verb)

1. a(n) + adjective + noun

    He is <u>a serious student</u> but <u>a hilarious comic</u>.

2. verb + adverb

    Karen <u>swims quickly</u> yet <u>talks slowly</u>.

3. prepositional phrase + prepositional phrase

    David eats <u>in the morning</u> and <u>in the afternoon</u>.

III. **Clauses** (groups of words that include a subject and a verb)

1. adjective clause + adjective clause

    Peter is a colleague <u>who teaches math</u> and <u>who conducts the orchestra</u>.

2. noun clause + noun clause

    I know <u>that you are smart</u> and <u>that you are nervous</u>.

- Connect similarly constructed sentences with paired conjunctions. Instead of two short sentences, always try to combine sentences. :

    Both … and (takes a plural verb)
    Both Susan and Jenny study Italian.
    Not only … but also
    Laura not only jogs but also lifts weights.
    Either … or
    Either the teacher or I am right.
    Neither … nor
    Neither the football players nor the soccer players take afternoon classes.

The subjects that come after the *but also, or,* and *nor* determine the verb.

> *Either the teacher or the **students erase** the whiteboard every day.*
> *Either the students or the **teacher erases** the whiteboard every day.*

When these pairs are used, they must be followed by parallel types of words, phrases, or clauses.

- Whenever possible, put as many words as you can before the conjunction.

Incorrect: I want either to go to Mexico and Brazil.

The sentence should read *I want to go to **either Mexico or Brazil**.*

■ Do not omit necessary words. Oftentimes omitted articles, auxiliaries, and prepositions affect parallel structure.

Incorrect: I always have and always will eat breakfast.

The sentence should read *I always have **eaten** and always will eat breakfast.*

Incorrect: Mark gave me an apple, pear, and oranges.

The sentence should read *Mark gave me an apple, **a** pear, and oranges.*

Incorrect: I was interested and surprised by the story.

The sentence should read *I was interested **in** and surprised by the story.*

Incorrect: The population of Japan is greater than Korea.

The sentence should read *The population of Japan is greater than **that of** Korea.*

Incorrect: Joanne is as tall if not taller than her sister.

The sentence should read *Joanne is as tall **as** if not taller than her sister.*

Parallelism Exercise 2

Make the following sentences parallel. In some cases, there may be more than one correct answer.

1. The apartment was beautiful, expensive, and had a lot of space.

2. If you're going to use this recipe, you'll need a pepper, onion, and tomato.

3. Our teacher is interesting: she plays piano, writes poetry, and is a painter of watercolors.

4. I always have and always will sing in the shower.

5. Please turn down the television, or will you go to sleep?

6. Michael hopes his dedication, ability, and that he is considerate will help him get the job.

7. Daniel is a happy child and sleeps soundly.

8. Jodie Foster is a great actress and directs movies well.

9. The books on the top shelf are older than the bottom shelves.

10. At the University of Pennsylvania, morning classes are far more popular than the afternoon.

Answers may vary. Here are some possible parallelism corrections for Exercise 1.

1. The apartment was beautiful, expensive, and **spacious**.

2. If you're going to use this recipe, you'll need a pepper, **an** onion, and **a** tomato.

3. Our teacher is interesting: she plays piano, writes poetry, and **paints watercolors.**

4. I always have **sung** and always will sing in the shower.

5. Please turn down the television or go to sleep**.**

6. Michael hopes his dedication, ability, and **consideration** will help him get the job.

7. Daniel is a happy child and **a sound sleeper**.

8. Jodie Foster is a great actress and **a good director**.

9. The books on the top shelf are older than **those on** the bottom shelves.

10. At the University of Pennsylvania, morning classes are far more popular than the afternoon **ones**.

Parallelism Exercise 2

Complete each of the following sentences by adding words, phrases, or clauses that are parallel to the italicized words. There are many possible answers.

1. I was in favor of either *painting the walls purple* or
   _____.

2. Matt found what he needed in the desk: *a ruler, a pen*, and _____.

3. The square was crowded with young tourists *studying their guidebooks, eating lunches from backpacks*, and
   _____.

4. Moving to a new apartment means I'll have to *decide what to keep, what to give away*, and
   _____.

5. During our coffee break we ate blueberry muffins that were *small* but _____.

6. The hats and coats were piled everywhere: *on the bed, on the chairs*, and even_____.

7. Bonnie knew neither *what to say in her letter of application* nor _____.

8. *Either the government will ban smoking in public buildings or* _____.

9. Molly walked *across the square* and

   _____.

10. In the morning newspaper I *read that plans for a second airport are being considered* and

    _____.

Answers may vary. Here are some possible parallelism corrections for Exercise 2.

1. I was in favor of either *painting the walls purple* or **leaving them alone.**

2. Matt found what he needed in the desk: *a ruler, a pen,* and **an old exam.**

3. The square was crowded with young tourists *studying their guidebooks, eating lunches from backpacks,* and **taking pictures of one another.**

4. Moving to a new apartment means I'll have to *decide what to keep, what to give away,* and **what to sell.**

5. During our coffee break we ate blueberry muffins that were *small* but **delicious.**

6. The hats and coats were piled everywhere: *on the bed, on the chairs,* and even **on the floor.**

7. Bonnie knew neither *what to say in her letter of application* nor **how to express herself effectively.**

8. *Either the government will ban smoking in public buildings or* **the people will revolt.**

9. Molly walked *across the square* and ***into the library.***

10. In the morning newspaper I *read that plans for a second airport are being considered* and ***noticed that the governor is opposed to the idea.***

Parallelism Exercise 3

Make the following sentences parallel. In some cases, there may be more than one correct answer.

1. After a day at the beach, the children came home tired, sunburned, and hunger.

2. Larry Bird was a quick, skillful, and energy basketball player.

3. A good writer edits her work slowly, carefully, and regular.

4. The English composition course contains short stories, a novel, and poetic.

5. When you write an essay, you should check each verb for agree, tense, and form.

6. The airline allows passengers to take one, two or third suitcases.

7. My mother has been a waitress, a secretary, and taught school.

8. My uncle spoke in a humorous way and with kindness.

9. I am hot, dirty, and need something to drink.

10. The flavor of the strawberry yogurt is better than the peach.

Answers may vary. Here are some possible parallelism corrections for Exercise 3.

1. After a day at the beach, the children came home tired, sunburned, and **hungry**.

2. Larry Bird was a quick, skillful, and **energetic** basketball player.

3. A good writer edits her work slowly, carefully, and **regularly**.

4. The English composition course contains short stories, a novel, and **poetry**.

5. When you write an essay, you should check each verb for **agreement**, tense, and form.

6. The airline allows passengers to take one, two or t**hree** suitcases.

7. My mother has been a waitress, a secretary, and **a teacher**.

8. My uncle spoke **with humor** and kindness.

9. I am hot, dirty, and **thirsty**.

10. The flavor of the strawberry yogurt is better than **the flavor of** the peach.

Parallelism Exercise 4

Make the following sentences parallel. In some cases, there may be more than one correct answer.

1. We want to have a flower garden, but we don't know where to begin, how to proceed, or the flowers we should plant.

2. The summer of 1950 was as hot, if not hotter than, any other in the last century.

3. I neither know what kind of computer he uses nor where he bought it.

4. I am afraid and excited about taking the TOEFL.

5. Jared has sent résumés both to graphic design firms in Taipei and Hong Kong.

6. Chris is an affectionate husband, a dutiful son, and kind to his kids.

7. The shape of the rock, how long it is, and the color reminds me of a small elephant.

8. He danced gracefully, rhythmically, and with ease.

9. Judy is a gifted woman: a biologist, does carpentry, and she can cook.

10. Your job consists of arranging the books, cataloging the new arrivals, and brochures have to be alphabetized.

Answers may vary. Here are some possible parallelism corrections for Exercise 4.

1. We want to have a flower garden, but we don't know where to begin, how to proceed, or **which flowers to plant**.

2. The summer of 1950 was as hot **as**, if not hotter than, any other in the last century.

3. I **know neither** what kind of computer he uses nor where he bought it.

4. I am afraid **of** and excited about taking the TOEFL.

5. Jared has sent résumés to graphic design firms in **both** Taipei and Hong Kong.

6. Chris is an affectionate husband, a dutiful son, and **a kind father**.

7. The shape of the rock, **the length**, and the color reminds me of a small elephant.

8. He danced gracefully, rhythmically, and **easily**.

9. Judy is a gifted woman: a biologist, **a carpenter**, and **a cook**.

10. Your job consists of arranging the books, cataloging the new arrivals, and **alphabetizing the brochures**.

4. Subject-Verb Agreement

■ Every complete sentence has a subject and a verb. The verb in every independent or dependent clause must agree with its subject. Although there is usually no problem in finding the subject and making sure it agrees with its verb, there are several exceptions and rules to learn.

■ **Prepositional Phrases that Come between the Subject and the Verb**

The verb is *not* affected by any prepositional phrase (*with, together with, along with,* etc.) that comes between the subject and the verb.

For example: The test *along with the answers* **is** found at the end of the book.

The subject, *test,* is singular. It agrees with the verb *is. Answers,* the object of the prepositional phrase *along with,* has no effect on the verb.

■ **There/Here**

In some sentences the verb comes before the subject. Be sure to find the entire subject.

For example: There **is** a lot of pollution in many countries today.

The subject is a singular noncount noun, *pollution.* It agrees with verb *is.*

For example: Here **are** a proposal, an outline, and a description.

The subjects are plural—*proposal, outline,* and *description. Here,* meaning they—the subjects—agrees with the verb *are.*

■ **Indefinite Pronouns or Adjectives**

The indefinite pronouns or adjectives *either, neither,* and *each* and the adjective *every* are always singular as are compounds such as *everybody, everyone,* and *someone.*

For Example: *Every* student, teacher, and employee **is** required to attend graduation.

- **Nouns Plural in Form** (ending in *s*)

Some nouns that end in -*s* require a singular verb. These nouns look plural, but they are singular in meaning.

COUNTRIES	EXAMPLE WORDS	EXAMPLE SENTENCES
Countries	Philippines, United States	The United States *has* fifty states.
		The Philippines *is* a FedEx hub.
School subjects	mathematics, economics, statistics, physics	Mathematics *is* required. Physics *is* taught in the afternoon.
Diseases	mumps, AIDS, SARS,	SARS *has* recently been diagnosed.
	measles	Measles *is* no longer common.
Other words	news, whereabouts	The news *is* on TV at 6:30 p.m..
		His whereabouts *is* unknown.
EXCEPTIONS (words that end in -*s* that are plural)	scissors, pants, glasses, jeans, gloves	My pants *are* too short. His glasses *are* from Korea.

Time, Distance, and Money

Time, distance, and money take a singular verb because the amount is considered a single unit.

For example: Six hours *is* a long time to wait for the bus.

Eight dollars *is* all you'll need for lunch.

Two miles *is* a lot to run every day.

Math Facts

These facts take a singular verb.

For example: Two plus two *is* four.

Eight divided by four *is* two.

Six times seven *is* forty-two.

Ten minus three *is* seven.

Gerunds as Subjects

Gerunds, nouns ending in -*ing*, always take a singular verb.

For example: Writing letters *is* no longer necessary.

The Number of/A Number of:

A number of means *a lot of* and takes a plural verb. *The number of* is used to give an exact amount and takes a singular verb.

For example: A number of teachers *are* sick today.

The number of days in a week *is* seven.

Languages/People

Nouns of nationality that end in *ch* (French), *sh* (Polish), and *ese* (Vietnamese) can mean either a language or a group of people. When used as a language, the noun is singular. When it's referring to people, the plural is used. Not all nationalities have these endings.

For example: Spanish *is* spoken in Mexico.

The Korean students in my class *speak* Korean during lunch.

Determining Modifiers

The nouns that follow the quantity words *some, all, part, most, fractions*, and *percents* determine the verbs. Don't be confused by the preposition *of*.

For example: Ten percent of the students *live* in apartments. The noun *students* is plural, so the verb *live* agrees with it.

Some of the money *is* in the bank. The noun *money* is singular, so the verb *is* agrees with it.

Collective Nouns

A collective noun names a group of people or animals. Although they do not end in *s*, they are plural and take a plural verb.

For example: The cattle *need* more grazing land.

The elderly *live* in nursing homes.

The rich *subsidize* this housing development.

Subject-Verb Agreement Exercise

Choose the correct form of the italicized verb.

1. Neither of the books that I ordered (*has, have*) come yet.
2. A number of students (*hopes, hope*) to graduate this June.

3. I can never remember if seven times eight (*is, are*) fifty-six or fifty-nine.

4. The president, with his wife, (*is, are*) planning to visit Hawaii.

5. Each of the students maintaining the required average (*is, are*) going to receive a scholarship.

6. Inside my pocketbook (*is, are*) my calculator, lunch, and keys.

7. Measles (*has, have*) reappeared among the kindergarten children.

8. The number of students in this year's freshman class (*is, are*) 212.

9. Eight miles (*is, are*) a lot to jog every day.

10. Indonesian (*is, are*) a very difficult language for Americans to learn.

11. The Dutch (*loves, love*) good bread.

12. The United States (*is, are*) more than two hundred years old.

13. Twenty dollars (*is, are*) a lot to spend for a pair of socks.

14. The news about the earthquake (*is, are*) surprising.

15. The police (*is, are*) exercising more nowadays.

16. Some of the students (*is, are*) taking an incomplete in the class.

17. Physics (*is, are*) taught by Dr. Roberts this term.

18. My scissors (*isn't, aren't*) sharp. Can I borrow yours?

19. Some of the lightbulbs from the kitchen (*is, are*) shining in my room.

20. Completing all the exercises (*is, are*) a good idea.

Subject-Verb Agreement Exercise Answer Key

1. has	11. love
2. hope	12. is
3. is	13. is
4. is	14. is
5. is	15. are
6. are	16. are
7. has	17. is
8. is	18. aren't
9. is	19. are
10. is	20. is

5. Pronouns

■ Pronouns are words that take the place of nouns or noun phrases. They refer to people or things that are previously mentioned in the sentence or that are understood from the context. Pronouns can serve different functions in a sentence. For example, they can serve as subjects or objects. The form of the pronoun usually changes depending on its function.

■ Recognize the function of the pronoun in the sentence.
  Be sure it is in the correct form.

SUBJECT PRONOUNS	OBJECT PRONOUNS	POSSESSIVE ADJECTIVES (must be followed by a noun)	POSSESSIVE PRONOUNS	REFLEXIVE PRONOUNS
I	me	my	mine	myself
you	you	your	yours	yourself
he	him	his	his	himself
she	her	her	hers	herself
it	it	its	*no form*	itself
we	us	our	ours	ourselves
you	you	your	yours	yourselves
they	them	their	theirs	themselves

For example: *The pronghorn resembles an antelope. It has small forked horns.*

It, the subject pronoun, refers to *the pronghorn* in the previous sentence. If the pronoun is the subject of the sentence, use a subject pronoun.

For example: *The horns are curved. Most animals are afraid of them.*

Them, the object pronoun, coming after the preposition *of*, refers to *the horns*. If the pronoun is the object in the sentence, use an object pronoun.

For example: *The job itself isn't so difficult. Carol lives by herself.*

These pronouns are reflexive pronouns, pronouns used when subjects and objects of a sentence refer to the same people or things. In the first sentence, *itself* refers to the preceding noun, *job*. In the second sentence, *by herself* means without any help or alone.

■ A pronoun must agree in number (singular or plural) with the noun it refers to.

Incorrect: By 1923 the average wage of industrial workers was twice what they had been in 1914.

The sentence should read: *By 1923 the average wage of industrial workers was twice what **it** had been in 1914.* The subject is *wage*, a singular noun, and the pronoun, *they*, is plural.

Incorrect: The kangaroo rat is so good at storing its seed supply in an underground burrow that farmers may someday borrow their method.

The sentence should read: *The kangaroo rat is so good at storing its seed supply in an underground burrow that farmers may someday borrow **its** method.* The pronoun *their* is referring to *the kangaroo rat*, which is singular.

■ Pronouns must be in the correct form.

Incorrect: The Double Helix is James Watson's notoriously personal account of the scientific feat that won himself and Frances Click the Nobel Prize in 1962.

The sentence should read *The Double Helix is James Watson's notoriously personal account of the scientific feat that won* **him** *and Frances Click the Nobel Prize in 1962.* The pronoun should be in the object form, not the reflexive one.

Incorrect: The telescopes of the late 1600s magnified objects 33 times theirs original size.

The sentence should read *The telescopes of the late 1600s magnified objects 33 times* **their** *original size.* The pronoun should be in the possessive adjective form, not the possessive pronoun form.

NOTE: Although you may hear students say, "Me and my sister are applying to graduate schools." The subject pronoun is needed. The sentence should read *My sister and I are applying to graduate schools.* (The pronoun needs to come after the named subject.)

NOTE: Make sure you use the object pronouns after prepositions. You may hear students say, "What I'm telling you is just between you and I." The sentence should read *What I'm telling you is just between you and* **me**.

- **If a sentence has a subject, it doesn't need a second one.**

  A pronoun is often used as an incorrect double subject.

  Incorrect: Puritan settlements they grew marvelously, as fur trading, fishing, and shipbuilding blossomed into important industries.

The sentence should read, *Puritan settlements grew marvelously, as fur trading, fishing, and shipbuilding blossomed into important industries.* The sentence has a subject, *settlements.* It cannot have a second subject, the pronoun *they.*

- **Avoid broad reference to this, that, which, and it.**

This, that, which, and *it* should refer to specific ideas and things rather than to whole sentences or clauses.

Incorrect: My father is a chemist. This is something I don't like.

The sentences should read *My father is a chemist.* **Chemistry** *is something I don't like.*

Incorrect: With the music blasting from the next room, Kimberly could not concentrate on *Ulysses*, which certainly irritated her.

The sentence should read *With the music blasting in the next room, Kimberly was irritated that she could not concentrate on Ulysses.* Her inability to concentrate is irritating her, not *Ulysses.*

- **Make sure the pronoun has a referent.**

Incorrect: In Kim's speech, she talked about her childhood.

The sentence should read *Kim talked about her childhood in her speech.* There is no reference for *she* in the incorrect sentence.

■ **Don't use the pronoun "*you*" in essays.**

■ ***Who, whom,*** **or** *whose* **refer to people;** *that* **and** *which* **do not.**

However, in conversation you will hear, "There is the boy that I told you about."

■ **Use the possessive pronoun or the possessive form of the noun before a gerund (-ing ending noun).**

Incorrect: Me getting an A was a surprise. Nicole getting an A was a surprise.

The sentences should read *My getting an A was a surprise. Nicole's getting an A was a surprise.*

Pronoun Exercise 1

Circle the pronouns. Draw arrows to the noun references. Then correct the errors.

1. Abraham Lincoln delivered its most famous address at the dedication of the soldiers' cemetery in Gettysburg.

2. The poet Marianne Moore was initially associated with the imagist movement, but later developed his own rhyme patterns and verse forms.

3. Many narcotic plants and its products, such as nicotine, are effective in controlling insects.

4. Farming becomes more expensive when farmers are forced to apply greater quantities of costly fertilizers to sustain its yields.

5. The metaphors we use routinely are the means by which we describe one's everyday experiences.

6. If they are prepared skillfully, soybeans they can be appetizing as well as nutritious.

7. Studies of both vision and physical optics began almost as early as civilization themselves.

8. James Whitcomb Riley, the "Hoosier Poet," wrote much of his work in standard English, but himself wrote his most popular poems in the dialect of his home state, Indiana.

9. A traditional Halloween decoration is a jack-o-lantern, which is a hollowed-out pumpkin with a scary face cut into them.

10. In the homeopathic remedy called *proving*, various substances are administered to healthy people and its effects carefully observed.

Pronoun Exercise 2 Answers/Explanations

1. <u>its</u>   *should be*   his   (to agree with *Lincoln*)

2. <u>his</u>   *should be*   her   (to agree with *the woman, Marianne*)

3. <u>its</u>   *should be*   their   (to agree with *plants*)

4. <u>its</u>   *should be*   their   (to agree with *farmers*)

5. <u>one's</u>	*should be*	our	(to agree with *we*)
6. <u>they</u>	*should be omitted*		(double subject)
7. <u>themselves</u>	*should be*	itself	(to agree with *civilization*)
8. <u>himself</u>	*should be*	he	(subject form)
9. <u>them</u>	*should be*	it	(to agree with pumpkin)
10. <u>its</u>	*should be*	their	(to agree with substances)

Pronoun Exercise 2

Of the four underlined choices, one is a pronoun error. Circle the pronoun error in each sentence and correct it.

1. The men and women <u>who</u> pushed the frontier westward across America probably <u>never</u> thought of <u>them</u> as brave pioneers.

2. The human brain <u>it</u> is <u>so highly</u> developed that it makes people <u>different</u> <u>from</u> all other living things.

3. The bottom of <u>a</u> valley is called <u>their</u> floor <u>which</u> usually slopes gradually <u>in</u> one direction.

4. <u>Most kinds of</u> mollusks, including clams and oysters, have a hard, <u>armorlike</u> shell <u>that</u> <u>protects</u> <u>its</u> soft bodies.

5. The <u>largest</u> crowds come to New Orleans for the <u>annual</u> Mardi Gras celebration, with <u>their</u> spectacular parades and <u>other</u> merry festivities.

6. <u>Most</u> bottom-dwelling creatures, <u>considered</u> part of the plankton, drift with the currents <u>during</u> the early stages of <u>its</u> development.

7. Porcelain, <u>characterized</u> by <u>its</u> whiteness and delicate appearance, is <u>a</u> type of ceramics highly valued for <u>their</u> beauty and strength.

8. <u>Manufacturers</u> of consumer <u>goods</u> often <u>change</u> the styles of <u>them</u> products.

9. <u>Inventor</u> Granville Woods received <u>him</u> first patent <u>on</u> January 3, 1984, for a <u>steam</u> boiler furnace.

10. Tent caterpillars <u>get</u> <u>its</u> name <u>because</u> most species spin <u>loose</u>, white, tentlike webs in the forks of trees.

11. <u>To form</u> a silicate glass, the liquid <u>from which</u> it is made must be cooled rapidly <u>enough</u> to prevent <u>it</u> crystallization.

12. <u>By</u> distinguishing <u>himself</u> as a judge in Arizona, Sandra Day O'Connor caught President Reagan's attention and <u>was appointed</u> the first woman justice <u>on</u> the Supreme Court.

13. The Postal Service has <u>modernized</u> <u>their</u> operations <u>to increase</u> the speed of mail <u>handling</u>.

14. Petroleum <u>it</u> is composed of <u>a</u> complex <u>mixture</u> of hydrogen <u>and</u> carbon.

15. <u>Archaeological</u> investigations indicate that control of fire is an extremely old technical attainment, though <u>the time</u>, place, and mode of <u>his</u> origin may never <u>be</u> <u>learned</u>.

16. The <u>hardness</u> <u>of</u> minerals often <u>gives</u> clues to <u>his</u> identity.

17. Taconite is <u>so</u> hard that <u>ordinary</u> drilling and blasting methods cannot <u>be used</u> to obtain <u>them</u>.

18. In the winter, New Hampshire skiers <u>race down</u> <u>snow-covered</u> slopes and then warm <u>them</u> near crackling fires in <u>friendly</u> ski lodges.

19. Gorillas are <u>the most</u> terrestrial of the great apes <u>because</u> their bulky size makes <u>it</u> ill-suited <u>to dwelling</u> in trees.

20. United States senators <u>were elected</u> by state legislatures until 1913, when the Seventeenth Amendment to the Constitution required that <u>them</u> be chosen <u>by</u> popular <u>election</u>.

21. Snails travel <u>on</u> roadways that they make <u>them</u> <u>by</u> <u>producing</u> a <u>sticky</u> liquid.

22. Tarragon is <u>widely</u> cultivated for <u>their</u> leaves and young <u>shoots</u>, which <u>are used</u> as a flavoring for vinegar.

23. Seeds <u>need</u> oxygen for the changes <u>that</u> take place within <u>theirs</u> during <u>germination</u>.

24. The two sides of <u>the</u> heart relax and fill, and then <u>contract</u> and empty <u>them</u> <u>at the</u> <u>same time</u>.

25. Profit is the <u>amount</u> of money a company has <u>left over</u> from the sale of <u>their</u> products after it has paid for all the expenses <u>of production</u>.

Pronoun Exercise 2 Answers/Explanations

1. <u>them</u>	*should be*	themselves	(reflexive)
2. <u>it</u>	*should be omitted*		(double subject)
3. <u>called</u> <u>their</u>	*should be*	called a	(no reason for possessive pronoun)
4. <u>its</u>	*should be*	their	(to agree with *kinds*)
5. <u>their</u>	*should be*	its	(to agree with *celebration*)
6. <u>its</u>	*should be*	their	(to agree with *creatures*)
7. <u>their</u>	*should be*	its	(to agree with *porcelain*)
8. <u>them</u>	*should be*	their	(possessive pronoun before noun, *products*)
9. <u>him</u>	*should be*	his	(possessive pronoun before noun, *patent*)
10. <u>its</u>	*should be*	their	(to agree with caterpillars)
11. <u>it</u>	*should be*	its	(possessive pronoun before noun, *crystallization*)

12.	himself	*should be*	herself	(to agree with *woman*)
13.	their	*should be*	its	(to agree with *The Postal Service*)
14.	it	*should be omitted*		(double subject)
15.	his	*should be*	its	(to agree with object, *origin*)
16.	his	*should be*	their	(to agree with *hardness*, a thing, not a person)
17.	them	*should be*	it	(to agree with *Taconite*)
18.	them	*should be*	themselves	(reflexive)
19.	it	*should be*	them	(to agree with *Gorillas*)
20.	them	*should be*	they	(subject form)
21.	them	*should be*	themselves	(reflexive form)
22.	their	*should be*	its	(to agree with subject, *Tarragon*)
23.	theirs	*should be*	themselves	(reflexive form)
24.	them	*should be*	themselves	(reflexive)
25.	their	*should be*	its	(to agree with singular noun, *company*)

Pronoun Exercise 3

Find pronoun errors in each sentence and correct them.

1. It helps people to get rid of something they don't want instead of throwing them away.

2. Everybody has to do what they are told to do.

3. In some countries, teenagers have jobs while themselves are students.

4. Between you and I, it's not a good idea to build a high school in my community.

5. I think universities should give more money to its libraries than to sports.

6. My best friend watches television all the time and doesn't spend enough time on hers homework.

7. I thought I knew a lot about the United States because I had seen many of their advertisements.

8. If I were to choose my roommate by myself, I might pick someone just like myself.

9. The invention of the telephone, it has enabled people in very remote areas of my country to feel less isolated.

10. Me and my best friend went to 10 countries together last summer.

Pronoun Exercise 3   Answer Key

1. It helps people to get rid of something they don't want instead of throwing **it** away.

2. Everybody has to do what **she is/he is/one is** told to do.

3. In some countries, teenagers have jobs while **they** are students.

4. Between you and **me**, it's not a good idea to build a high school in my community.

5. I think universities should give more money to **their** libraries than to sports.

6. My best friend watches television all the time and doesn't spend enough time on **her** homework.

7. I thought I knew a lot about the United States because I had seen many of **its** advertisements.

8. If I were to choose my roommate by myself, I might pick someone just like **me**.

9. The invention of the telephone has enabled people in very remote areas of my country to feel less isolated. (omit **it**)

10. **My best friend and I** went to 10 countries together last summer.

6. Who/Whom

- **Who** and **whoever** are used for subjects and are subject complements. **Whom** and **whomever** are used for objects and are object complements. Look at the clause itself, not what comes before it. If you can replace the *who/whom* with *he (she/they)*, use *who*. If you can replace the *who/whom* with *him (her/them)*, use *whom*.

For example: Give the ticket to ***whoever/whomever*** is at the desk. Use **whoever** because you can say, *"he is at the desk."*

For example: The adviser **who/whom** I was assigned to meet for lunch. Use **whom** because you can say, *"I was assigned to him."*

■ Use **who/whom** when there is a linking verb (*be, seem, appear,* etc.) in the clause.

For example: I wonder ***who/whom*** she is. Use **who** because of the linking verb **is (she is she)**. After a linking verb, the pronoun is in the nominative/subject case/form. The sentence should read, *I wonder who she is.*

■ Be careful of the verbs *know, think, says,* and *believe* when they come between the **who/whom** and verb.

For example: John, ***who/whom*** I know will be elected president, is a friend of mine. Use **who** because the clause is really, "He will be elected president." Ignore the *I know*.

Who/Whom Exercise

Circle the correct answer.

1. Each of the women who / whom danced on the green at Marlott that fine day doubtless had enough private drama in her life to fuel a novel.

2. I met a person who / whom you would like.

3. The teacher who / whom read my paper liked it.

4. Who / whom do you think called me last night?

5. Who / whom won the swim meet?

6. Ask whoever / whomever is at the desk for help.

7. I know who / whom you look like.

8. Although Angel did not dance with Tess, it was she who / whom Angel remembered as he walked away from Marlott that day.

9. Tess was among the girls who / whom presented themselves as dance partners.

10. Give dinner to whoever / whomever is at home.

Who/Whom Exercise   Answers

1. Each of the women **who** danced on the green at Marlott that fine day doubtless had enough private drama in her life to fuel a novel.

2. I met a person **whom** you would like.

3. The teacher **who** read my paper liked it.

4. **Who** do you think called me last night?

5. **Who** won the swim meet?

6. Ask **whoever** is at the desk for help.

7. I know **whom** you look like.

8. Although Angel did not dance with Tess, it was she **whom** Angel remembered as he walked away from Marlott that day.

9. Tess was among the girls **who** presented themselves as dance partners.

10. Give dinner to **whoever** is at home.

7. Sentence Variety

■ Using a variety of sentence structures will make your writing seem advanced and enjoyable to read. You may be writing sentences that are grammatically correct but boring because they all sound and look the same. As you look over your essays, check to see if many of your sentences begin with *I* + a verb. Do you often connect clauses within your sentence by using only *and*? As you concentrate on improving your writing, try to change the types of sentences and sentence structures that you use.

For example: Look at this SUBJECT + VERB sentence:

I cooked every night at home. I hoped to become a great chef.

■ You could instead begin with a *gerund phrase*.

By *cooking every night at home,* I hoped to become a great chef.

■ Or you could use a *participial phrase*.

Cooking every night, I hoped to become a great chef.

■ Or you could use an *infinitive phrase*.

My only hope of becoming a great chef was *to cook every night*.

■ Or you could begin with a _prepositional phrase_.

> _With nightly homecooked meals,_ I hoped to become a great chef.

■ Or you could use an _appositive phrase_.

> I decided that there was only one way to become a great chef: _nightly homecooked meals_.

■ Or you could use a question.

> _How could I become a great chef?_ I could begin by cooking at home every night.

■ Or you could use connectors.

> _Compound sentence:_ I cooked every night at home, _for_ I hoped to become a great chef.
>
> _Complex sentence:_ I cooked every night at home because I hoped to become a great chef.

Strategies

■ **Use an occasional question.**

■ **Make sure you're not beginning all sentences the same way, such as I + a verb.**

■ **Don't write all simple sentences. Look at your writing to see where you could connect two simple sentences and create one compound or complex sentence.**

■ **Use the above-mentioned phrase variations.**

Grammar

Sentence Variety Exercise

Rewrite and combine these sentences written by nonnative speakers.to make them more interesting. Feel free to add words and related ideas.

1. I wore a uniform every day. I hated it.

   _____

2. I've lived in five countries. I tried to dress and act like the native people.

   _____

3. I've learned many things on my own. I learned how to ride a bicycle by riding one, not by reading about it.

   _____

4. In my country, university students don't have to go to class. Teachers don't care whether or not students come.

   _____

5. I played soccer in high school. My team didn't win one game.

   _____

6. I have many friends and go out with them on the weekend. I like to be alone during the week.

   _____

7. I grew up in a modern 22-story apartment building. I want to live in a traditional house.

   _____

8. I would like to visit Australia. I could never afford to go there.

   _____

9. Some people listen to music when they are sad. Some people listen to music when they are in a good mood.

   _____

10. I live in a very boring small town. I wish we had a movie theater in town.

   _____

Answers will vary. Here are some possibilities to improve the sentence variety.

1. I had to wear a uniform every single day, and you have no idea how much I hated it.

2. I've lived in five different countries, always trying to dress and act like the native people.

3. Although some people learn better from a manual or a teacher, I'm the kind of person who learns by doing, such as when I learned to ride a bicycle.

4. In contrast to what I've heard about some institutions in the United States, in my country teachers at the university level don't care whether or not students come to class.

5. Unfortunately my high school soccer team didn't win even one game.

6. Although I like to be alone during the week, I look forward to going out with my many friends on the weekend.

7. Maybe because I grew up in a modern 22-story apartment building, I want to live in a traditional house.

8. Although I could never afford to visit Australia, I'd certainly like to visit there.

9. Some people like to listen to music when they're sad; whereas others like to listen when they're in a good mood.

10. My hometown is so small and boring that it doesn't even have a movie theater!

8. Dangling and Misplaced Modifies

- Modifiers (words, phrases, or clauses) that describe other words should point clearly to the words they modify. In general, related words should be kept together.

Misplaced Modifiers

- Don't split infinitives.

Incorrect: I want to never see him again.

The sentence should read, *I want **never to see** him again.* Although you will hear the incorrect form in conversation, don't use it in writing.

■ Adverbs such as *only, even, almost, nearly*, and *just* should come right in front of the word they modify.

Incorrect: I only ate half the pie.

The sentence should read, *I **ate only** half the pie.* Again, you may hear the incorrect form. Be careful in your writing.

■ Phrases and clauses should appear next to the words they are modifying.

Incorrect: I wrote my thesis at Harvard on the destruction of Pompeii in 1997.

The sentence should read, *I wrote my thesis **at Harvard** in 1997 on the destruction of Pompeii.* The destruction of Pompeii was not in 1997.

■ Don't place adverbs between two verbs.

Incorrect: The woman who had been dancing gracefully entered the room.

The sentence should read either, *The woman who had been **gracefully** dancing entered the room.* OR, *The woman who had been dancing entered the room **gracefully**.* Was she dancing gracefully or entering gracefully?

Dangling Modifiers

■ When a sentence begins with a phrase, the subject of the independent clause should be the same. Either (1) change the subject of the independent clause to agree with the subject of the phrase, or (2) change the phrase to a dependent clause.

Incorrect: When only three years old, my father took me to see *The Man with the Golden Gun*.

You can correct this sentence in two ways: (1) *When only three years old, **I went with my father** to see* The Man with the Golden Gun. (2) ***When I was only three years old**, my father took me to see* The Man with the Golden Gun.

Incorrect: Barking all night, the owners put the dog outside.

You can correct this sentence in two ways: (1) *Barking all night**, the dog had to stay** outside*. **(2) *Because the dog barked all night**, the owners put the dog outside.*

Dangling and Misplaced Modifiers Exercise

Rewrite the following sentences. If a sentence is correct, write CORRECT.

1. Using my computer, the report was finished in two days.

2. Sarah fed the dog wearing her pajamas.

3. Short of money, the trip was canceled.

4. Typing as fast as she could, Hannah could not wait to finally finish her paper.

5. The pigeons were fed sitting in the park.

6. I noticed Samantha walking down the hall quietly eating an apple.

7. Working overtime, my salary almost doubled.

8. Lucas only looked at the man sitting in the chair with the red hair.

9. Dressed professionally, Sean was not nervous about the interview.

10. Stepping on the brakes, my car would not stop for the red light.

Answers will vary. Here are some possibilities.

1. Using my computer, **I finished** the report in two days.

2. **Wearing her pajamas**, Sarah fed the dog.

3. Short of money, **I canceled** the trip.

4. Typing as fast as she could, Hannah could not wait **to finish** her paper **finally**.

5. **Sitting in the park, I fed** the pigeons.

6. I noticed Samantha walking down the hall eating an apple **quietly**.

7. Working overtime, **I almost doubled** my salary.

8. Lucas looked **only** at the man **with the red hair** sitting in the chair.

9. Dressed professionally, Sean was not nervous about the interview. **CORRECT**

10. **Although I stepped** on the brakes, my car would not stop for the red light.

C. Grammar Posttest

Correct all the errors in the following sentences. The errors focus on the topics covered in the grammar appendix: sentence fragments, run-on sentences, parallelism, subject-verb agreement, pronouns, who/whom, sentence variety, and dangling/misplaced modifiers. If the sentence is CORRECT, write C.

1. Sitting in the back of the room, it was difficult for Daniel to see the blackboard.

2. With a mysterious smile, Leonardo da Vince painted the *Mona Lisa*.

3. I told the employment agency that I did not want to be a typist because I do not enjoy it.

4. When someone blocks caller ID, you don't know whom is calling.

5. I hope to never again stay up all night studying for a test.

6. I decided to wear a shirt to school which had all its buttons.

7. The substitute today whom used to teach at MIT now teaches at Harvard.

8. The secret I'm about to tell you is just between you and I.

9. The iPod was a gift from her best friend which was in a pink case.

10. There are also a system of cables connected to all the buildings.

11. Every Tom, Dick, and Harry want to go to Las Vegas.

12. The student who answers all questions soon will receive extra credit.

13. Susannah getting all the answers right on the homework was surprising.

14. Because I wanted to learn Spanish.

15. Don't forget to give your essay to whomever is working in the writing center.

16. Chosen to light the Olympic torch, we were delighted to see Mohammed Ali on the platform.

17. My neighbor's new grandson almost sleeps through the night.

18. This test will be as hard if not harder than the one from last semester.

19. I was afraid and shocked at his behavior.

20. On her desk was a dictionary, an index card, and a pencil.

21. Despite her dermatologist's warnings, Lily always has and always will lie in the sun.

22. You can either take this review seriously, or you can be disappointed with your score.

23. I'm planning on reviewing all the homework exercises. I'm retaking all the old quizzes. I'm making up Jeopardy questions and answers to use in class.

24. Whitney said that when she tried on the jeans how glad she was that she had grown two inches.

25. I studied really hard for the midterm, I got a really good grade.

26. Both gemstones and stars shines.

27. Neither my history teacher nor my zoology teacher answer all the questions correctly.

28. Most of the books that we choose provokes some lively discussion.

29. It is difficult for we mortals to guess what profound impact a simple choice makes.

30. A dancer's legs are more muscular than a writer.

Corrections are in BOLD. The grammar rule of the error and the rule number are marked. Some sentences may have more than one possible answer.

1. **Because Daniel sat** in the back of the room, it was difficult for **him** to see the blackboard.

   Dangling/misplaced modifiers (8)

2. Leonardo da Vinci painted the *Mona Lisa* **with a mysterious smile.**

   Dangling/misplaced modifiers (8)

3. I told the employment agency that I did not want to be a typist because I do not enjoy **typing.**

   Pronouns (5)

4. When someone blocks caller ID, you don't know **who** is calling.

   Who/whom (6)

5. I hope **never again to stay** up all night studying for a test.

   Dangling/Misplaced modifiers (8)

6. I decided to wear to school a shirt **which had all its buttons**.

   Dangling/misplaced modifiers (8)

7. The substitute today **who** used to teach at MIT now teaches at Harvard.

   Who/whom (6)

8. The secret I'm about to tell you is just between you and **me**.

   Pronouns (5)

9. The iPod **which was in a pink case** was a gift from her best friend.

   Dangling/misplaced modifiers (8)

10. There **is** also a system of cables connected to all the buildings.

    Subject-verb agreement (4)

11. Every Tom, Dick, and Harry **wants** to go to Las Vegas.

    Subject-verb agreement (4)

12. The student who answers all questions will receive extra credit **soon.**

    Dangling/misplaced modifiers (8)

13. Susannah**'s** getting all the answers right on the homework was surprising.

    Pronouns (5)

14. Because I wanted to learn Spanish, **I vacationed in Mexico.**

    Sentence fragments (1)

15. Don't forget to give your essay to **whoever** is working in the writing center.

    Who/whom (6)

16. **Mohammed Ali was** chosen to light the Olympic torch, and we were delighted to see **him** on the platform.

    Dangling/misplaced modifiers (8)

17. My neighbor's new grandson **sleeps almost** through the night.

    Dangling/misplaced modifiers (8)

18. This test will be as hard **as** if not harder than the one from last semester.

    Parallelism (3)

19. I was afraid **of** and shocked at his behavior.

    Parallelism (3)

20. On her desk **were** a dictionary, an index card, and a pencil.

     Subject-verb agreement (4)

21. Despite her dermatologist's warnings, Lily always has **lain** and always will lie in the sun.

     Parallelism (3)

22. You can either take this review seriously **or be** disappointed with your score.

     Parallelism (3)

23. I'm planning on reviewing all the homework exercises before the test. **Retaking** all the old quizzes will help me to prepare. **By making** up Jeopardy questions and answers to use in class, **I'll be prepared.**

     Sentence variety (7)

24. When she tried on the jeans, Whitney said **how glad she was that she had grown two inches.**

     Pronouns (5)

25. I studied really hard for the midterm; I got a really good grade.

     Run-on sentences (2)

26. Both gemstones and stars **shine.**

     Subject-verb agreement (4)

27. Neither my history teacher nor my zoology teacher **answers** all the questions correctly.

     Parallelism (3)

28. Most of the books that we choose **provoke** some lively discussion.

    Subject-verb agreement (4)

29. It is difficult for **us** mortals to guess what profound impact a simple choice makes.

    Pronouns (5)

30. A dancer's legs are more muscular than are a **writer's.**

    Parallelism (3)

Appendix II Punctuation

A. Punctuation Pretest

Insert the necessary punctuation. The errors focus on the topics covered in the punctuation appendix: the comma, semicolon, colon, apostrophe, quotation marks, end punctuation, and title punctuation. If the sentence is CORRECT, write C. There may be more than one error per sentence.

1. I transferred to Mount Ida College, because I wanted to major in forensics.

2. I quit my part-time job, therefore, I have more time to help students than I did before.

3. What I need to buy for my room are: a quilt, a desk lamp, and an alarm clock.

4. The dog licked it's paw after being stung.

5. One of my favorite proverbs' is, "Don't cry over spilt milk".

6. I really enjoyed our summer reading assignment, *The Old Man And The Sea*.

7. I need a new advisor, and will get one who advises interior design students.

8. The tax rate in the United States is 29 percent; the tax rate in Japan is 32 percent.

9. Students, who wish to retake the math placement test, must pay $10.00.

10. Professor Martin, who teaches EN101, is my advisor.

Corrections are in BOLD. The punctuation rule relating to the error and the rule number are marked.

1. I transfered to Mount Ida **College because** I wanted to major in forensics.

   Comma rules (1)

2. I quit my part-time **job;** therefore, I have more time to help students than I did before.

   Semicolon rules (2)

3. What I need to buy for my room **are** a quilt, a desk lamp, and an alarm clock.

   Colon rules (3)

4. The dog licked **its** paw after being stung.

   Apostrophe rules (4)

5. One of my favorite **proverbs** is, "Don't cry over spilt milk**."**

   Apostrophe rules (4)   Quotation mark rules (5)

6. I really enjoyed our summer reading assignment, *The Old Man **a**nd **t**he Sea*.

   Rules for capitalizing titles (8)

7. I need a new **advisor and** will get one who advises interior design students.

   Comma rules (1)

8. The tax rate in the United States is 29%; the tax rate in Japan is 32 percent. **CORRECT**

   Semicolon rules (2)

9. **Students** who wish to retake the math placement **test** must pay $10.00.

   Comma rules (1)

10. Professor Martin, who teaches EN101, is my advisor.
    CORRECT

    Comma rules (1)

B.   Punctuation Rules

1.   Comma (,) Rules

■ Do not use commas (,) between two sentences (see run-on sentences Appendix I).

■ Use commas before coordinating conjunctions (*for, and, nor, but, or, yet, so*) if there are a subject and a verb before and after the conjunction.

   For example: *I like black and wear black clothes a lot.*

   I like black, and I wear black clothes a lot.

■ If you have three adjectives, verbs, or nouns in a row, separate them with commas.

For example: *I like black, brown, and turquoise.*

■ If an adjective clause comes after a person's name, you can set it off with commas. These adjective clauses are called nonessential clauses. By using commas, the reader knows that the information is *not* essential to the meaning of the sentence.

For example: *Jeff Brown, who lives next door to me, works in my office.*

The man who lives next door to me works in my office.

In the second sentence I do not know who the man is, so I don't use commas. In the first sentence, the adjective clause is *extra* information about Jeff Brown.

Incorrect: Students, who arrived on time, may leave early.

I don't mean *all* students. I mean *only those who arrived on time*, so I cannot use commas. The sentence should have no punctuation. *Students who arrived on time may leave early*.

■ Use commas to set off introductory adverbial clauses. If the clause is *not* at the beginning, don't use a comma.

For example: *Because I was sick, I stayed home.*

I stayed home because I was sick.

2. Semicolon (;) Rules

▪ Use a semicolon between closely related independent clauses that are not connected to a coordinating conjunction (*for, and, nor, but, or, yet, so*).

> For example: *The tax rate in the United States is 27 percent; the tax rate in Japan is 32 percent.*

NOTE: Do *not* use the semicolon often as a way to combine sentences. The sentences must be very clearly related.

▪ Use a semicolon with transitional adverbs (*however, therefore, consequently, moreover, nevertheless, nonetheless, thus, hence,* etc.). Put a semicolon (;) before them and a comma after them if there are a subject and a verb before and after.

> For example: *I (**Subject**) like (**Verb**) black; therefore, I (**Subject**) wear (**Verb**) it a lot.*

> Also correct: *I (**Subject**) like (**Verb**) black; I (**Subject**), therefore, wear (**Verb**) it a lot.*

3. Colon (:) Rules

▪ Use a colon only after a complete sentence and before a list, an appositive, or a quotation.

> For example: *I took many things to the beach: a blanket, suntan lotion, and lunch.*

The car advertisement glorified one of the deadly sins: greed.

Accept the words of Maya Angelou: "Success is liking yourself, liking what you do, and liking how you do it."

4. Apostrophe (') Rules

- Apostrophes to show possession are usually used for people (Emily's room), but sometimes they are used for objects, as in, "All in a day's work."

1. If the noun (singular or plural) does not end in s, add 's.

   For example: *man's men's child's children's*

2. If the noun is singular and ends in s, add 's.

   For example: *Phyllis's schedule*

3. If the noun is plural and ends in s, add only an apostrophe (').

   For example: *The students' names.*

4. For joint possession, use an apostrophe with the second name.

   For example: *John and Greg's brother* (one brother)

5. To show individual possession, make all nouns possessive.

   For example: *John's and Greg's scores were very different.*

- Use an apostrophe (') to show omission in contractions.

    For example: *It's* (It is) *good news.*

- Omit the apostrophe in the plurals of numbers and decades.

    For example: *The 1960s were a turbulent decade.*

5. Quotation Mark Rules

- Do not use quotation marks in the titles of essays.

- Use quotation marks for *direct* quotations. Do *not* use quotation marks for *indirect* quotations.

    For example: She asked, "How much does the TOEFL cost?"

    She asked how much the TOEFL cost.

6. End Punctuation

- Make sure you end each sentence with either a period, exclamation point, or question mark.

- Do *not* begin sentences with periods, commas, question marks, or exclamation points.

7. Rules For Punctuating Titles

- Do not use quotation marks in the title of an essay.
- Always capitalize the first word.

■ Do not capitalize articles (*a, an, the*), coordinating conjunctions (*for, and, nor, but, or, yet, so*) or prepositions (*in, on, at*, etc.) *unless* these words are the first word in the title.

> For example: *The Old Man and the Sea; Six Weeks on a Desert Island.*

■ Capitalize all major words such as nouns, pronouns, verbs, adjectives, and adverbs.

■ It's okay to ask a question, followed by a question mark.

For example: Should Students Evaluate Teachers?

C.   Punctuation Posttest

Insert the necessary punctuation. The errors focus on the topics covered in the this appendix: the comma, semicolon, colon, apostrophe, quotation marks, end punctuation, and title punctuation. If the sentence is CORRECT, write C. There may be more than one error per sentence.

1. Although Jessica was absent she e-mailed me asking for the homework.

2 There are three sections on the final exam multiple choice short answer and a long essay.

3. I got autographs from my three favorite movie stars Meryl Streep Jodie Foster and Robin Williams and I screamed for joy.

Punctuation

4. Jean-Claude has taken several English classes therefore he is confident about his writing ability.

5. Benjamin Franklin supposedly said be civil to all, and enemy to none.

6. Samantha who lives out-of-state explained in her essay why she prefers to live in a dorm.

7. The famous last three lines from The road not taken a poem by Robert Frost are, Two roads diverged in a wood, and I—I took the one less traveled by, And that has made all the difference.

8. Carmens daughter was sick so Carmen took her to the doctor.

9. I've been teaching for five years but have never had a student from Utah or New Mexico before this semester.

10. Taylor was worried about the midterm and thought about it during the break.

11. After Diana came to one class she never appeared again.

12. Luis speaks several languages Portuguese Spanish English and Italian.

13. I arrived on time for the test however I forgot my learners permit.

14. Classes which meet on Monday evenings will meet an additional time during exam week.

15. !Bravo! If I call your name you passed the entrance examination.

Corrections are in BOLD. The punctuation rule relating to the error and the rule number are marked.

1. Although Jessica was absent, she e-mailed me asking for the homework.

   Comma rules (1)

2. There are three sections on the final exam**:** multiple choice, short answer, and a long essay.

   Colon rules (3) Comma rules (1)

3. I got autographs from my three favorite movie stars**:** Meryl Streep, Jodie Foster**,** and Robin Williams, and I screamed for joy.

   Colon rules (3) Comma rules (1)

4. Jean-Claude has taken several English classes**;** therefore, he is confident about his writing ability.

   Semicolon rules (2)

5. Benjamin Franklin supposedly said, **"B**e civil to all **and** enemy to none."

   Quotation rules (5) Comma rules (1)

6. Samantha**,** who lives out-of-state, explained in her essay why she prefers to live in a dorm.

   Comma rules (1)

7. The famous last three lines from **"**The **R**oad **N**ot **T**aken**"** by Robert Frost are, **"**Two roads diverged in a wood,

and I- I took the one less traveled by, And that has made all the difference."

Rules for capitalizing titles (8) Quotation mark rules (5)

8. Carmen's daughter was sick, so Carmen took her to the doctor.

Apostrophe rules (4) Comma rules (1)

9. I've been teaching five years but have never had a student from Utah or New Mexico before this semester. **Correct**

Comma rules (1)

10. Taylor was worried about the midterm and thought about it during the break. **Correct**

Comma rules (1)

11. After Diana came to one class, she never appeared again.

Comma rules (1)

12. Luis speaks several languages: Portuguese, Spanish, English, and Italian.

Colon rules (3) Comma rules (1)

13. I arrived on time for the test; however, I forgot my learner's permit.

Semicolon rules (2) Comma rules (1)

14. Classes which meet on Monday evenings will meet an additional time during exam week. **Correct**

     Comma rules (1)

15. Bravo! If I call your name, you passed the entrance examination.

     End punctuation (6)